HOLDING ON FOR LIFE

JEFF R. BROOKS

HOLDING ON FOR LIFE

credo
house publishers

Holding on for Life
Copyright © 2014 by Jeff Brooks
All rights reserved.

Published in the United States by Credo House Publishers, a division of Credo Communications, LLC, Grand Rapids, Michigan
www.credohousepublishers.com

ISBN: 978-1-625860-08-8

Editing by Donna Huisjen
Cover and interior design by Frank Gutbrod

Printed in the United States of America

First edition

CONTENTS

Introduction 1
Preface 5

PART 1
1   *To Start at the Beginning* 9
2   *Rebellion* 19
3   *Salvation, Beer and Romance* 25
4   *Chasing Love* 35
5   *Marriage and the Military* 41
6   *Denial and Alcoholism Explained* 49
7   *Progression of Addiction and Moral Culpability* 55
8   *Hope Within the Storm* 65
9   *Breakdown . . . or Breakthrough?* 75
10   *Emerging From Darkness* 81
11   *Gaining Traction* 97
12   *Marriage and Family* 107
13   *Prosperity and Growth* 113
14   *The Trial* 121
15   *Graduate School* 129

PART 2

16	Longing for More	141
17	I Need a Job	147
18	All Hell Breaks Loose	153
19	Searching for Home	159
20	Launching the Next Phase	171
21	Out the Gate	177
22	Timing Is Everything	183
23	Tiger by the Tail	189
24	My Dark Night of Sense	195
25	Putting It All in the Rearview Mirror	203
26	Closure	207

About the Author 213
3 Days Rising 215

INTRODUCTION

I am the fortunate recipient of a life well lived. It isn't a life that I designed, and certainly not one I shaped at the onset of conscious awareness. It's a life crafted by a power greater than myself—a divine love that has breathed upon my soul from the onset of my existence. A providential hand of protection and provision. An intimate ally of my heart. This is the source of my life—the narrative behind *who I am* and *why I am*.

This isn't to say that I was detached from or negligent about engaging in a life plan. I had dreams from as far back as I can remember. Dreams to succeed, to excel in love, romance, meaning and power. To be helpful and to make a difference.

But I quickly learned that I lived in an intensely painful world. This awareness fought against my innocence and my hopes. There was in this world no end of abuse—meanness and violence, fear and shame. Things weren't as they seemed, and I often experienced intense loneliness and isolation. And all of this within the confines of a single zip code! What could the rest of the world possibly be like?

I was to stumble upon alcohol as a salve for my pain—a temporary clarifier of my reality (or at least I thought so). I was destined to succumb to the seduction of this idol. Addiction had held a hereditary status in my family for many generations. The surrounding environment supported this lifestyle, as there was little structure or outside scrutiny to check my proclivities. My aunt was mentally impaired and my mother simply busy and tired. There was no one about with the awareness, willingness or influence to intervene. My early reliance upon alcohol led to dependence within a short two years. I was barely functioning enough to finish the 11th grade, and I dropped out of school afterward, only to acquire a GED and enter the workforce at the age of 17. For 13 more years I would find myself sucked into the vortex of a progressive downward spiral of mental, spiritual, emotional and physical degradation that stripped my soul of hope, crushed the life from any potential accomplishments and hurtled me toward a destiny of destruction and death.

This isn't to say there weren't several times throughout this period when I sought help and attempted to exercise my faith, imploring God to remove the burden of insanity from me. And there were brief periods of reprieve, invariably followed by devastating seasons of relapse. My recovery would be a process, not an event. Still, I held on to an unquenchable love for God and a determination to find freedom.

All of this information is included here to provide context; it isn't designed to evoke sympathy or to inject the "drama" at which today's young so scoff. Each one of us experiences our own private series of wounds to the heart. They arise from many different sources, but the diverse themes blend to form an undeniable plot to each of our lives. As contemporary Christian author John Eldredge puts it, "The story of your life is the story of the long and brutal assault by an enemy who knows who you can be and fears you."

These facts I share frame the experience of a young boy whose life was oppressed and assaulted. As the narrative progresses, it is revealed that Jesus wins this one back.

And as He does, you'll come to recognize that the account is meant to be encouraging, inspiring, helpful and hopeful. If I've permitted myself to linger in the distortion—in the pain, the suffering and the loss along the way—I will have misrepresented not only what has happened but also the consequences of those events. No, the truth and the hope lie in the interpretation, as God has indeed worked all things together for my good. I have learned two important things through my journey:

1. that God is who He Says He is and
2. that He will do what he says He'll do.

Thank you for reading this book. I have committed my effort toward good stewardship of your time and interest. It's my sincerest desire that you'll find hope and encouragement in my story—that you'll gain from it additional insight into the intimate and pursuing heart of God. Because pain in the human experience is universal, I'm confident you'll find similarities in your own experience. However, because we are all beautifully and wonderfully made, no two of us alike, there will be inevitable differences. Please don't let these dissimilarities distract you. As an old saying from Alcoholics Anonymous goes, "Don't compare, just identify." I'm confident you'll find that this approach can open many insights applicable to your own journey of self-discovery and freedom.

PREFACE

The scene unfolds with a backdrop from the movie *Dances With Wolves*. There is sun, open sky and flowers; waist high, an expansive prairie unfurls in all directions. There's an adult holding my hand, and we're walking in a relaxed and conversational manner. I'm four years old, and for the first time in my young life I feel peace and safety—an enveloping sense of love and wellbeing. I know who this man is, even though He has never mentioned His name. I can't make out anything He's saying, but I sense that the reality of the scene is how it has been, is and is to be: that I belong for eternity in a place that was made for the essence of who I am.

I awaken to realize that this has been a dream. Still, despite my tender age at the time, this memory has been embedded and intractable, anchoring my soul through all of the tumultuous, tragic and comedic rhythms of my life.

I've always felt as though God's hand was on me—that He was somehow covering me with His favor. I don't know how I came to know this any more than I remember the background of knowing where my house is, who my brother is or where to find the cereal. It's just there and I know it.

I realize this kind of assertion makes some folks uncomfortable. It may sound to them as though I'm declaring "I'm special" or "I have it and you don't, so there must be something wrong with you." But that isn't it. I take no credit, possess no special attributes that allow me to both know of and receive this reality. Yet as you read along I believe you'll see and agree that:

a. I'm an unlikely recipient of God's revelation and grace. He found me because of who *He* is.
b. You and I are special, loved for who He created us to be and thus eligible to receive this grace.
c. We aren't alone.

PART 1

1

TO START AT THE BEGINNING

And so it began, in 1961, when I appeared on the scene as the youngest of four in a family recently dispersed by the assault of alcoholism and divorce. North Charleston, South Carolina was like any other Southeastern town in the early sixties—tense with racial division, an unwinnable war looming in the near future, and an ostentatious display of disproportionate prosperity lightly veiling oppressive poverty and despair.

My mother was a high school dropout. What she lacked in education, though, she more than compensated for in character. Her fierce determination to care for her children proved to be an eternal flame that on many occasions illuminated the difficult path of her life.

My emergence on the scene was preceded by the arrival of three older siblings—all at a considerable chronological distance from my debut: a brother who was eight years my elder, a sister who was then 12 and the oldest—another brother—then aged 15. This extensive age difference seems to suggest that I may not have been a part of the family plan. Especially considering that the "last straw" seems to have been pulled by my thoroughly frustrated mom just prior to my birth, I can only assume that my conception was the result either of a last-attempt "make up" or an impromptu encounter. Either way, my arrival into the Brooks family must have been an inconvenient intrusion, as there was little emotional and financial structure to support a new baby.

The household consisted of the aforementioned siblings and two additional hangers-on—an aunt and my grandfather. My mother had actually moved in with these two, along with her brood of three and, of course, I was eventually born into the household. All of us managed to squeeze ourselves within the limited confines of a two bedroom, 800-square-foot house.

Growing up as the youngest of four children, my worldview was characterized by suspicion, fear and uncertainty. My caretaker was my mother's sister—an undiagnosed paranoid schizophrenic who was functional enough to come off as "a little eccentric," while dependent enough to have to live with us (again, lest I misspeak myself, *we* were the latecomers). Her unconventionality, however, was also a foundation for her creativity. She loved to draw and often told me fascinating stories at bedtime, in which cats and other animals were personified in fantastical accounts of adventure. This process no doubt helped cultivate my own creativity, instilling in me an ability to visualize the abstract and the unseen.

My mother, the divorcée of a severe (is there any other kind?) alcoholic, worked two and sometimes three jobs to keep the family in provisions. She was for the most part away from home, as were my siblings. For all practical purposes I grew up an only child, although she would go on to serve for me as a beacon of hope, love and encouragement in ways that I did not fully appreciate until late adulthood. I had no better ally in my foxhole. She had a way of loving me through the most difficult times in my life, while still holding me accountable to a higher standard. She expected the best from me and saw my potential and talents long before I could.

There were periods during which we were all in the same room at the same time, but more often our house was comprised of empty bedrooms populated during occasional drop-in visits, usually coinciding with holidays, when we looked to the outside world as though we were at least distantly related. My earliest memories of childhood include four seemingly random but significant events:

1. A vague display of fondness from my grandfather. He would hold my hand and give me the "secret grip," a slight squeeze that made me feel loved, safe and special.
2. A late-night disruption near the front door when one of my brothers would come crashing in as though he were being pursued by the dark riders from The Lord of the Rings trilogy. Apparently there was yet another racial riot unfolding just down the street and an angry mob moving in our direction. I recall my mother grabbing the shotgun and keeping vigilance by the entryway, reinforcing for me that danger was always nearby and ready to pounce. Bad "ju ju" out there.
3. An encounter with some guy I came to later know as Jesus. More on this later.
4. Romance—somewhere in my early childhood experience I learned that a girl could warm my heart and make me feel differently about myself. A pervasive sense of inadequacy skewed my self-identity, and only the proximity of a pretty girl would relieve it. I experienced my first rejection of true love when my kindergarten sweetie refused to play on the model truck I had just wrestled from my buddy. This initiated what

would prove to be a lifelong pattern of thievery and rejection contributing to an overall moral decline.

The sixties, as we know, were a time of chaos and unrest in the Southeast. Racial divide was evident in my neighborhood elementary school, where forced and enforced compliance with the new segregation law created an atmospheric tension among teachers and confused students alike. An underlying and at times latent rage pervaded the classrooms and playground. As a timid young boy, I found myself continuously trailed by inadequacy and fear. I couldn't seem to shake the belief that I was somehow different from other people and therefore "wrong."

Still, I delighted in the daily routine that was my life. The egocentric world of childhood fosters wonder, hope, excitement and joy. We have yet to come to terms with our limitations, and the world has yet to evoke its stain of fear and anxiety. Santa Claus and the Easter Bunny still held sway in winter and spring; Captain Kangaroo provided unfailing instruction and wisdom through my black-and-white television set; and an afternoon snack of applesauce, despite the accompaniment of an unwanted nap, provided a semblance of predictability to my weekday afternoons.

The two years I spent in kindergarten (just half a block down the street) introduced me to new friends and the concept of an outside world. There were snowmen and trucks, coloring books and lessons on writing. There was infatuation with a cute little girl named Tammi, whose presence somehow rendered me acutely self-aware. My failure to allure her in the direction of mutual affection reinforced my nascent sense of inadequacy. It still amazes me to recall experiencing this at such a young age. I believe I can with some certainty observe the formation of sensitivity in my young soul—a sensitivity that provided insight but also exacted payment in emotional pain.

This pain was exacerbated by childhood sexual abuse. The perpetrator and details of this aspect of my history are secondary to the impact. Thousands of people could fill in the blanks, with all of our stories culminating in the same general outcome—shame, confusion, fear and anxiety. This kind of early experience wreaks havoc on an innocent soul by exploiting the attachment bond to another human being. Left behind is a pervasive sense of "something wrong with me," along with an obsession to be validated by something worthwhile or good. Something has been stolen and remains missing. The obsession to fumble our way back to that original identity leads many to the brink of self-destruction.

Grade school revealed an aptitude for learning, particularly in the area of reading. It also exposed the intensity of the shame and inadequacy that had taken hold from the sexual abuse. I was competent in the classroom but avoidant on the playground. When physical education became part of the curriculum, I worked diligently to come up with some excuse not to participate. My caretaker aunt was an accomplice in this, her views of school and authority deeply skewed by a suspicion grounded in untreated schizophrenia. She would write bogus notes to the teacher to excuse me from participation—notes I learned to "edit" to avoid expiration dates. This compulsion to avoid required dishonesty—another character trait that began to emerge. Manipulation of others to get what I wanted, or prevent something I didn't, soon followed.

I found ways to compensate for my lack of presence and prowess on the playground. Taking my natural sense of humor and the creativity to apply it to another level, I would frequently bring levity to the classroom and sarcasm and wit to my peers.

I had to be careful in terms of how far I took this because of my small size and physical ineptness. I could easily insult the wrong guy, one who failed to appreciate the intricacies of my humor, and suffer retaliation at recess time.

These attributes also found their way into my writing. When the subject of personification was introduced to our English composition class, I discovered a passion for bringing inanimate objects to life. My work would often be held up as an example to the other students. On occasion either I or the teacher would read aloud my contributions to the class, an exercise often followed by laughter and appreciation. My public speaking life began to take shape.

When something like this "works"—when we encounter a positive response from others to an action or behavior—we're inclined to hone in on this and refine the experience for replication. When such satisfaction alleviates the sense of loneliness and inadequacy, the aptitude moves beyond a mere asset and becomes an essential survival tool. I had long ago decided that I wasn't "enough" as a person. If I were to be safe and loved I would need to bring something to the relational table. Humor and wit provided for me a persona of confidence, allowing me to fit in. I had something to offer. I mattered.

Church attendance became part of my early childhood routine. I was baptized in the Anglican tradition at the age of six, and my aunt and I attended an Episcopal Church in downtown Charleston. This was an experience of high church in all aspects—incense, rich liturgy, chanting and hymnals. It was inspiring, but I felt somehow emotionally distant. Still, I held zealously to the revelation that Jesus was good, and the weekly attendance provided me both with a structure and an emerging faith in a powerful God.

I became an acolyte at this church and through weekly exposure to the liturgy perceived the beauty and awe that were attributed to God and His Son. The old Scottish priest (Samuel Fleming) took me under his wing and invariably seemed to have encouraging and kind words to say to me. His grandfatherly manner impressed upon me that some men could in fact be both good and safe. Father Fleming was the first of several influential men God was to provide for my journey. He would often affirm me with predictions like "Jefferey, you will make a fine priest someday!" My confirmation at age 12 seemed to validate that church and a life of faith were certainties that could be acquired even in the midst of an unstable childhood.

Reflection and Application Exercises

I believe it is no accident that you have picked up this book. That said, I encourage you to find out why.

Prayer and meditation are ancient practices that have been proven to help us learn, grow and heal throughout the narrative of our life. This process is a discipline that allows us to engage our truest self for the purpose of reviewing our motives and actions, while giving us the time and space to unpack all that is going on in our hearts. I encourage you to pursue this endeavor, using whatever increments of time you can work into a schedule. Some people are better in the mornings, others in the evenings. But *you* must make it happen, knowing that there will always be an inconvenience, intrusion or disruption.

Pick a quiet place. If you're new at this, start with just five minutes. You can add to this weekly. Ideally, if you can work up to thirty minutes you'll get the most from the experience. Don't feel guilty if this proves challenging—just get started!

The questions that accompany these chapters are designed to help stimulate thoughts and discussion surrounding your own life experiences. You can use a journal or a working notebook to jot down thoughts, feelings and insights that may arise. I suggest that you keep this journal or notebook in a place where you know it won't be read by anyone else. This will eliminate any felt need to "edit" your thoughts and feelings. You can always choose later on to either share or not share this information. It is first and foremost between you and God.

There are some action/application suggestions as well, some of which you may find helpful. But please don't dismiss them until you've tried.

Reflection Questions

The author's formative years and the context of his early family life are illustrated in this chapter. During these earliest years our deepest and most abiding messages about ourselves, the world, God and others are inscribed upon our hearts. These have a way of shaping our beliefs, attitudes and values.

1. What was your childhood like?
2. What did you do on holidays?
3. What feelings arise in your heart when you reflect back on those times?
4. What are some sad or negative early events that shaped your life?
5. What are some happy or positive experiences that made a difference early on?

Application Exercise (you can use a journal or just a working notepad):

Write down or discuss five adjectives or feelings that best describe your childhood. If this were to have a title, like a chapter in a book, what would you call it?

2

REBELLION

When my siblings moved on, the household consisted of my absentee mother, my aunt and myself. The routine of church life slipped away. My early adolescence was characterized by a rebellious attitude. I had left the public school system for a Catholic middle school (my guardians' attempt to shelter me from the evil world about us) and found that my wit and oppositional nature scored many social points with my Catholic schoolmates. I became the class clown—the long-haired Protestant boy who could skirt some of the rules and bring laughter to a stoic culture. Anger began to replace fear. My sarcasm was a veiled attempt to strike out against someone—an unspecified and all too inclusive "someone"—for all of my fear and confusion in life. The scars of early childhood fomented an irritation within my soul, along with an intense desire to act out.

I felt more real and alive just knowing I had the ability to steal or vandalize something, and the act itself produced a pronounced sense of strength and confidence. My cohort of deviant friends admired my courage and abilities, kindling in me the determination to keep on doing it, despite an aching conscience that tried to warn me off the dangerous path toward self-destruction.

I was becoming a different person.

The "false self" is a fairly common psychological term to describe one's attitudes, beliefs and behaviors that are contradictory to their true values. That "self" adheres to a learned set of character traits that have become ingrained as a result of deep-seated vows they've made along the way. These vows can also be known as "agreements." The agreements will essentially pair off into the subcategories of mandates or injunctions. A mandate insists that "I must always believe or do something." For example: "I must always look after myself!" An injunction states "Don't trust anyone else." The character traits that evolve from these agreements provide safety or bring relief to the areas of our lives that crave validation, security, power and success. They can be considered instinctual and form a catalyst for our desires, or they can be become the orange cones of our journey—guiding us around self-perceived obstacles and danger. Frustration is the subjective experience of failing to reach some objective or goal. This might involve something materialistic (a new car), safety (a secure neighborhood to live in), basic provision (food), accomplishment (a promotion at work), esteem ("She's a great friend!") or certitude (financial security). There are other possibilities, of course, but these categories reflect the sources of much of our frustration.

All of these are highly influential areas of our lives. Robert Maslow, an influential social psychologist, pursued exhaustive and conclusive research he later developed into a theory called—you guessed it—Maslow's Hierarchy of Needs. Its illustration follows:

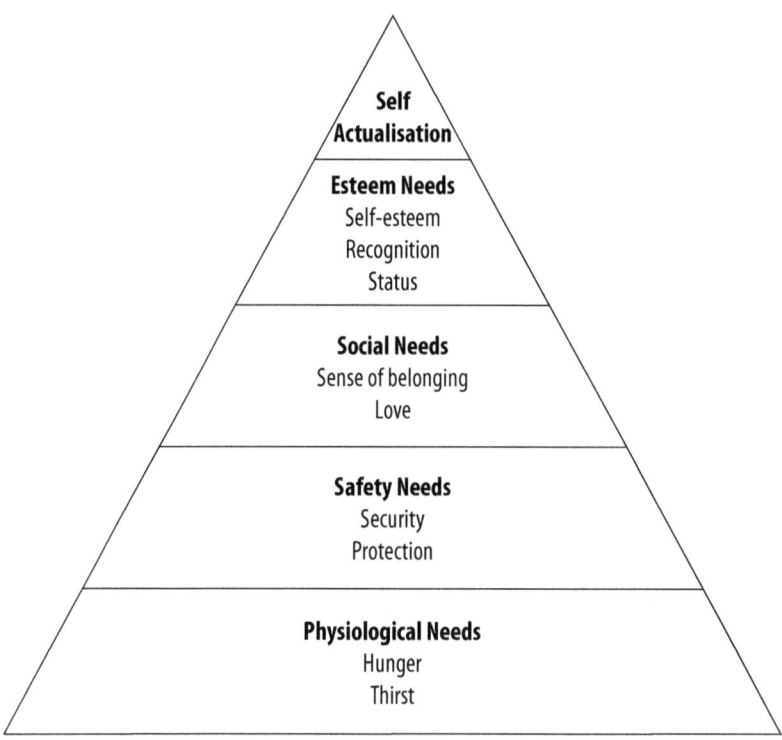

It's evident for us as human beings that these needs are engrained in our psyche and manifested in our attempts to navigate life. We can't be faulted for that!

But notice something more intriguing in this tension: we experience frustration in these areas of life because at the core of our reality and in our reflective anxiety we're acutely aware of the following truths:

a. There's no certainty in this world.
b. It's a lonely business trying to arrange for everything to work out.
c. Life is tiring.
d. Life is frustrating.

What to do about this? I believe we can easily fall into the counterfeit pursuit of happiness to replace the deeper virtue of joy when we determine that:

a. Life is a big disappointment.
b. God is holding out and won't provide for me, or He's indifferent to my desires, or there is no God, or I shouldn't expect too much from Him.
c. It's up to me to find life, to make it happen.
d. And therein lies the agreement: *If it is to be, it is up to me.*

I lived this out. I could enter a retail store and quickly determine that I could get away with taking whatever it was I wanted. On one occasion, in a daring exhibition of shoplifting expertise, I actually pulled an entire retail display from the ceiling. The chain, attached to the ceiling mount on the one side and a stain-glassed Coca Cola sign on the other, carried a significant amount of weight. It must have been a display model, because it was firmly rooted to the tile ceiling. As the fixture came tumbling down, creating a horrific din, I managed to slide it into my coat. The staff and customers knew, of course, that something had happened—just not what or how. My poker face, followed by a "What are *you* lookin' at?" expression of challenge, deterred further inquiry. I made it out with my loot and a solid reputation (among those whose opinions on such things mattered to me) as a top-notch thief. This was the stuff of childhood legend and the embodiment of my false persona. I was—to use the official terminology—a bad ass.

Reflection Questions

The early adolescent years are a time of confusion for many kids. We try to fit in with our peers while at the same time seeking our individual, identity, away from the family system. We "try on" a variety of different personas, and the emergence of the "false self" is common.

1. What were your teenage years like?
2. Describe five feelings that come to mind from your recollection of that time.
3. Who, or what, did you try to become in those years?
4. What were your greatest dreams?
5. What were your deepest fears?
6. What "mandates" came from this time in your life? (Hint: you will recognize these as those things you feel compelled to do even when you don't want to.)
7. What injunctions developed during this time? (Hint: you will recognize these as things you avoid.)

3

SALVATION, BEER AND ROMANCE

I was living a double life. My "bad boy" attitude grated against an aching sensitivity in the direction of those things I knew to be good and true. I longed to belong and couldn't find lasting comfort in either lifestyle. Ironically, the evangelical outreach of a local church would only serve to strengthen this antagonism.

My first genuine experience with salvation came at the age of 13. A conversation with my evangelistic neighbor resulted in an honest conviction of my personal need for a Savior, along with clarification of who Jesus is and why He came to Earth. I knew *of* Jesus already but hadn't connected the salvation implications until this discussion. Fully convinced, I accepted Christ into my heart and experienced the warmth of assurance that something big had just happened. I was excited and even did some evangelizing with my friends and schoolmates. The turnaround felt genuine and true and . . . for a while, provided a clarity and purpose I had never known before. The man gave me a small Bible and met with me on occasion to discuss the rising questions of my heart.

It was also around this time that I affiliated with a local Southern Baptist congregation. While my aunt had dropped out of Episcopal church attendance (and picked up witchcraft instead), my sister had found Jesus at the corner church and was serving as a youth group volunteer. She would pick me up three times a week to attend the services, and I actually enjoyed connecting with other teens in this context. Sitting through the numerous and lengthy services, though, the trajectory of my spiritual formation began to shift. I learned that God was actually pretty mad at us—mostly because we sinned. I couldn't disagree with that—I was sinning in all sorts of obvious ways. In fact, I was fully aware of my sins and vowed every morning to stop them, only to fall back into these patterns by lunchtime.

The solution, according to the pastor, was to invite Jesus into my life. I had done this already, but apparently it hadn't stuck. During one of these services I felt that compelling spirit of conviction and responded to the invitation at the altar. It became apparent, however, that regardless of this decision I would need to frequently respond to the altar call as a "backslider." Since I was doomed to continue life as a worthless sinner—despite having been saved by grace—it seemed as though God were going to have to stay mad at me after all. Discouraged, I determined that I just couldn't keep up with the ritual.

Hindsight reveals that my formative transition from knowledge of and desire for God to a personal relationship with Him (through salvation) had once again been assaulted. My enthusiasm was replaced by confusion and a sense of abandonment. Disillusioned, I drifted away from my youth group and clung to others who seemed to share in my dilemma. I had an uncanny knack for connecting with the spiritually distressed and slightly antisocial—the outcasts and the rebels, with whom I felt a natural affinity.

A part of this heart assault can be attributed to two key events in the summer of 1975. As I merged into the vulnerability of early adolescence, I made a random trip to stay with my sister outside of Jacksonville, Florida. Back then the summer seemed endless, and I carried with me the mental construct of a boy who still liked to play, explore the woods and pretend to be a cowboy or a cop. I was holding on tenuously to that fleeting season of boyhood naiveté.

The setting was a small farm in a rural area of Clay County. The area had once boasted horses and cattle, and my sister's "in-laws" lived across a pasture. There were two girls and a boy, all close to my age. We hit it off immediately and spent the seemingly endless summer days playing, exploring and doing the stuff kids do at that age.

This was a magical time for me. I rode a horse, shot a rifle, played cops and robbers, explored the woods and fields and just got to be a kid. I had a major—and happily reciprocated—crush on one of the girls and even experienced my first real kiss. I felt fully alive!

Second, and for no ostensible reason that I can understand even now, my biological father was introduced to me. Or, I should say, imposed upon me. Evidently he was passing through the area, and plans were arranged for him to come by and see me. I had never before met the man and frankly hadn't given him much thought. After 12 years on Earth and no prior exposure to this side of the parenthood equation, I had built my reality on a "no dad" approach, which seemed to work fine for me. The thought of meeting this guy, in fact, terrified me. My new friends seemed to understand my fear and were readily supportive.

The day arrived when this mystery man was to come to my sister's house. I was out playing, immersed in one of those random pick-me-up games that kids are so good at improvising when I was beckoned to the house and led into the living room. Peering gingerly around the corner I slowly entered, only to behold a very large man lying immobile on the couch. Gone. Snoring, heaving his chest . . . and drooling. Big guy with a red face. Ugly as hell, honestly.

I turned imploringly to my sister, who was behind me looking almost apologetic. We left the room without any verbal exchange; nothing needed to be said—the man was passed out in a drunken stupor. I engaged in some brief conversation with an uncle and aunt I'd never met (apparently traveling with him) and left the house. If there was any conversation with my estranged father I've blotted it from my memory. I just felt disgusted, disappointed and unaccountably shamed.

I tried to fall seamlessly back into my new world of friends and innocent play. This worked wonderfully for all of another couple of weeks, after which my nascent romance with the neighbor girl caught the attention of her parents. Unbeknownst to our loving hearts, a plan was formulated to whisk me back to Charleston. With only a few hours' warning I was informed (as was she in a separate meeting) that I would be leaving the next day. What had been planned as an endless, 12-week visit was abruptly torpedoed by that nebulous "change of plans" that can so ruthlessly govern a child's helpless world. We kids were permitted to say our goodbyes, and she and I promised to write and stay in touch—to somehow make "it" all work out. Somehow, please, . . . *somehow!*

I remember only too well the long ride out of town and back home. Past the skating rink, the ice cream shop, the places we had shared over that short season of bliss. The Beatles' "Ticket to Ride" blared on the car stereo—"I think I'm gonna be sad I think it's today, yeah." Music always seemed to articulate what I couldn't.

My defenseless heart was crushed.

Beer Is Good

This ongoing emotional state, coupled with relentless peer pressure, finally eroded my self-determination to refrain from the use of alcohol or drugs. On Easter weekend of 1977 I conceded to the enchantment of a counterfeit god. Alcohol infused me with an immediate sense of power, control, security and that elusive sense of belonging for which I had so long searched. The first drink coincided with my first experience of intoxication. This led to a conviction that *this* was the solution to all my problems, the answer to all my questions, the reliable source of everything I would ever need. This is the lie of every idol, and it epitomizes the hope of every wounded soul that *something, anything*, has come to save the day.

Alcohol abuse became more than an encounter with euphoria—it provided meaning. I now stood for—and belonged to—something. My new allegiance constituted both a philosophy and a religion. I could now enter into "fellowship" with the party crowd, who passionately viewed life as one big extravaganza. Carelessness and an ingrained attitude of indifference were the accepted codes of life. The more adventure and booze, the more orthodox the belief. I can recall seemingly countless experiences of reckless driving, driving under the influence, and late night encounters with bad guys and spooky people. I should have been maimed or killed in my adolescence. Yet I felt a bravado and camaraderie with this subculture that seemed to fill the hole in my soul. I felt like a man.

And a real man needs a woman by his side, right?

"My Best Friend's Girlfriend," a popular song of the late 1970s, was my mantra. The allure of "stolen goods" added an additional value to my quest. Lori was a childhood friend who used to attend the same Episcopal church I did. My buddy dated her and we often drank in the same circles. When he left the area to go out West for employment, I immediately connected with her at a romantic level. Within six months we had actually made a feeble attempt at running away together, a proposition interrupted in its early implementation by law enforcement. I was now the bad guy, forever banished from her by the protective parents.

I had long been a romantic at heart, always dreaming of finding the perfect love and lifelong partner. I would daydream on this fantasy for hours. Music often provided the canvas on which I could project my poetic longings upon some futuristic but destined relationship. Every encounter with a girl led to the existential question of my existence—"Is she THE ONE?"

No wonder I frequently ended up on the rejected side. This approach is desperate and intimidating, even smothering. Fits of jealousy and fear would eventually seep out into conversations, with the self-fulfilled prophesy of abandonment never far behind. I would invariably find myself dumped, left, rejected. The pain, no matter how anticipated, was always excruciating. I was a moth drawn irresistibly to light and then thrust into a dark spiral of suffering and emasculation. Alcohol "helped" me cope but created a cyclical pattern of discovering and embracing helpless and manipulative girls.

The end with Lori was the same as all those other endings to follow. She hooked up with one of my best friends, and the happy couple proceeded to taunt me with continual displays of public affection. Attending a small high school added depth to what had begun as a puncture wound to my heart. My friends witnessed my betrayal on the most public of stages. I looked and felt like a loser. Never mind, though: I could and would drown myself in booze.

Susan was the rebound. I'm not exaggerating when I state that she captivated many of us with her beauty. My best friend from childhood dated her for nearly a year; once again, we socialized and walked in the same circles. She had witnessed my recent loss of Lori and consoled my heart through our friendship. During the course of one of her frequent and prolonged arguments with my buddy David, he confided in me that he would be breaking up with her for good. That was all the invitation I needed. I asked whether I could date her—more of a courtesy request than a genuine appeal for permission. He threw me an odd look and a bravado-laden "Fine with me!" Nonetheless, that incident would mark the end of our long-term friendship and the initiation of my reputation as a traitor.

Susan and I quickly grew in our commitment to each other. My budding alcoholism was still masked at this point, and the first year mirrored much of what a relatively normal teenage romance should be. Not surprisingly, her parents were suspicious of me—and wisely so. But the two of us lived out a deep commitment that might have rivaled that of Romeo and Juliet. My destined lover had finally arrived, and I was determined to have her. Possessiveness, fanned by insecurity, reared its ugly head. My entire being was consumed by my felt need for her.

This, I realize through the lens of retrospect, isn't love. If you're reading observantly, you'll detect the qualities of a narcissistic and possessive man, one whose entire identity is invested—subsumed, even—in the woman of his dreams. This is a setup for all sorts of relational pathology, including criminal domestic violence. Fortunately, God's grace held me back from overt aggression, but my anger and insecurity manifested themselves through every other category of abuse—emotional, psychological and spiritual.

My mother witnessed the self-destructive choices I was making but could do nothing about them. This would prove to be a pattern for my life over the next 13 years. It's hard to imagine the emotional and psychological pain this must have caused her. Yet she maintained an unconditional loved for me. It is no exaggeration that children can be cruel—sometimes unintentionally so—to their parents at times.

Susan and her family (she was a junior in high school) relocated to Indiana in the fall of 1979. I could no longer tolerate the confines of an academic schedule and had dropped out of school, somehow acquiring a GED (Graduation Equivalency Diploma). Working at a local pizza joint, I set my sights on joining her in Indiana and waiting out her graduation. We would then marry and live the life for which we mutually longed. I did in fact follow through on the relocation, my alcoholism stowed neatly and unobtrusively within my soul.

Reflection Questions

Some people grow up in and around a church community. Others have little or no family tradition in this regard. When questions and beliefs about God come up in conversation, we often hear many different interpretations of and opinions about sin, judgment, behavior, belonging and believing.

1. Was your family of origin involved in a church or faith community? If so, who participated and who didn't? What degree of commitment or understanding was manifested by those who did? If you had no religious upbringing, what was important in your family? What held a high value?

2. What were the beliefs in your family about God? About what life is all about?
3. What were your experiences with alcohol and/or drugs?

4

CHASING LOVE

Indianapolis represented a serious leap into reality for a small-town Charleston boy. I was excited to be on my own in a place where anonymity, not to mention promiscuity, could thrive. Setting up a one-bedroom flat within an easy two-mile trek to the local Pizza Hut (my place of employment), I had everything I needed to launch my new life. I would await my future bride's graduation from high school with no other intentions or thoughts about life, its purposes or meanings.

In the restaurant business a subculture exists that revolves around the ever-changing shift work and collective encounters with many people living on the moral fringes of society. I'm not intending in any way to disparage this vocation, which does offer numerous advantages and can in fact be noble work. However, I gravitated to the group that worked the later shifts, emerging after 2:00 a.m. to blend into the already active nightlife. My small apartment served as a convenient location for myself and others to get "smashed" until the sun began to rise.

My tolerance for alcohol and all night binging allowed me to drink and rave with the toughest of partiers. Other drugs were used, but alcohol was always my staple and drug of choice. Given the "right" circumstances, infidelity was easily conceded, sometimes several times a month. I worked hard to maintain a double life, to mask from my girlfriend my frequent intoxication and dishonesty.

I hadn't yet discovered that certain types of alcohol produced a distinct and dangerous response in my system. Ironically, it turns out I can't tolerate liquor very well. Something inside my psyche turns violently antisocial with the consumption of hard spirits. I also experience blackouts.

A blackout is a phenomenon of chemically induced amnesia, in which an intoxicated person can function somewhat normally but lacks the capacity for short-term memory. This kind of behavior is robotic and highly unpredictable. Alcoholics are frequent victims, and the aftereffect is a terrifying awareness of the amnesiac experience. The blackouts are also evidence of alcohol abuse evolving into intractable alcoholism.

My first experience of this occurred on an early Sunday morning. The prior events were fairly routine—worked until 2:00 a.m. and then met friends at the apartment for drinks, music and rowdiness. Someone passed around some tropical concoction, along with a somehow hilarious caution regarding potential flammability. At 18 one lacks the sense or experience to know better than to drink highly flammable liquid. Remember, I never had a dad to tell me otherwise—not that he would have, based on my single experience with (or of) him, had he been in the picture. Being orphaned in this way isn't only sad but can be dangerous. In retrospect, I'm speculating that the main ingredient of this beverage was grain alcohol. The problem with friends like this is that they disregard all legal requirements to post a nutritional label on their product.

I recall "coming to" to find myself walking behind a mall. The crackle of a police radio and the sudden appearance of a cruiser alerted me not only that something was happening but that I was in the middle of it. I quickly darted around a dumpster, gained my bearings and ran through backyards to make it home.

I never did find out what had happened, but I knew for sure that this blackout thing scared the hell out of me. I didn't even have a term for it—just knew this wasn't normal and made a decision to cut back on the partying stuff.

To my credit, I spent the next six months trying to control my behavior, but I always ended up conceding to a drink based on some unrealistic rationalization that I could handle it. Thus began a long period of attempting to control my problem: adjusting the drink composition, smoking either more or less marijuana, taking more or less of the other types of proffered pills. I had an emerging but vague sense that I might be depending on this stuff too much. I could go several days without using; ironically, I was always aware at this point that I felt a little better. However, the craving and obsession would quickly return, and I would binge. I had the capacity to stay awake for days at a time and still function. This propensity would quickly catch up with me, though. I got fired from my job, and most of my friends avoided me due to my frequent intoxication and unpredictable behavior. Susan knew I had a problem, but I always diverted her scrutiny by reinforcing my love and devotion to her.

I believed my own lies.

Susan's family got transferred back to Charleston the next year, and I in pursuit made the escape back to my hometown. This geographical change was met with general enthusiasm. My life had become unmanageable in Indiana, and everyone around me knew it. I desperately hoped to make another new start. Another apartment, another job at Pizza Hut and a brief stab at vocational school followed.

It took another year for Susan to finish high school. During this interim before we were able to get married, she got pregnant. We knew her family would retaliate in a strong fashion, so, following a course of misinformation and immature decision-making we moved to solve our problem through an abortion.

The law was such that she could consent to the procedure without parental notice. I honestly can't recall the preliminary thoughts and feelings associated with this, but I all too clearly remember my deep regret afterward. I brought her back to my apartment for a brief respite, during which I waited on her solicitously. Susan was physically sick for several days afterward, but I had as yet no idea what this experience was doing to us spiritually and emotionally. Something in our moral fiber shifted, as sand has a way of doing on a declining slope. There was a pervasive sense that something bad had happened—something we were loath to label, if we acknowledged it to one another at all. For my part, I attempted to cover up all the dissonance in an ongoing use of alcohol and drugs. I had learned early on how to distance reality when it threatened to become uncomfortable or intrusive. This time was no exception.

We responded in the only way confused and immature people do to such a stressful situation—we tied the knot.

Reflection Questions

Learning to love and to be loved is one of the most difficult experiences of life. We all long to know someone intimately and to be known in the same way. Our core desire to be accepted hinges on this dynamic.

1. What was the name of your first love?
2. What emotions did you experience during this time in your life?
3. How did this relationship end?
4. What messages came to you through this experience?

Application Exercise

Take some time and reflect on the themes of your relationships, specifically your romantic ones. What drew you toward each person (if there was more than one)? How would you describe the people with whom you connected? Was there a place in you that felt *completed* by being in their presence? Does a painful memory linger in this area of your life?

If so, make a note of this reality. It can serve as a basis for learning more about yourself. Consider bringing any unresolved issues to God. Talk about them with a trustworthy person.

MARRIAGE AND THE MILITARY

We chose December 28, 1981, for our wedding day. A rural Episcopal church would provide the religious credibility for our commitment, while my buddies supplied the essential items needed for a legitimate, pagan-style bachelor party. I state these recollections in the same sentence because they held approximately equal priority in my mind—first to get plastered and then to fulfill my romantic quest to capture the beauty. I always have had a knack for multi-tasking.

We started our married life in a small apartment. While Susan worked I cooked pizzas and attended vocational school for TV and radio repair. This season of our lives eventually led to her dismayed discovery that there was more distortion in my life than just my drinking. She had uncovered my fidelity problems.

I was at this point still able to keep some of this masked by deliberate confusion and misunderstanding. Unfortunately for her, she was desperate enough to accept this guise at some level. I didn't like what was happening to me when I drank. My behaviors were escalating at an alarming rate in terms of unpredictability.

I would wake up at 2:00 in the morning, at times with an overwhelming desire to go out and drink. This would lead to some quick scheming, followed by sneaking out of the bed and into her purse for the car keys and some cash. My intention was to grab a few drinks and laughs with some of my single buddies and crawl back into bed before she awoke. By 6:00, though, I no longer cared and was carelessly willing to expose my conspiracy as a "dammit all to hell" reaction to life. My ability to hold a job, as well as to keep up with the school vocation, dissolved on the basis of my drunkenness and unreliability. My poor bride watched her dreams dissipate with every drinking binge. In unintentional cruelty I would go for days and even a week at a time doing well, only to break out in a binge of obsessive-compulsive drinking, followed yet again by that deceptive and mutually destructive rebound to "normalcy." The whole cycle was insanity.

In our second year of marriage we left our apartment for a small rental house in a nearby county. Reconstructing our lives, along with another geographical change, brought more optimism. I recall being able to stop drinking for a record nine days—only to celebrate this accomplishment with a huge binge.

It was during one of these escapades that I was first arrested for driving under the influence. Borrowing a car, I left the house in search of some drugs to enhance my drinking ability. I recall getting to Charleston and meeting with the dealer but lost memory until I was back in Summerville, South Carolina, just a few blocks from what we then called home. At this point I remember being pulled from the car by a deputy and noticing with surprise that the vehicle was lodged in a ditch. I was told the next day that I had tried to outrun the patrol car and was making good progress until I hit the ditch. Ironically, this disclosure provided me with some unreasonable sense not only of satisfaction but of genuine manhood.

What was truly remarkable in this event is illustrated by my response to the arrest. I had wrecked someone else's car and no doubt put lives in jeopardy; yet I was thoroughly miffed that my mother wouldn't come and bail me out of jail. I vaguely remember going on some sort of verbal tirade as I insisted upon her need to stop what she was doing (translated as leaving her place of employment) and bring the cash *now, dammit!* The sad truth is that by this point I was sober and still acting like this, a delusional, narcissistic self-centeredness replacing my alibi of intoxication. A self-perpetuating, self-sustaining system of denial, entitlement, obsession, rationalization and compulsion was exposing itself to everyone but me. I was mentally ill and had no clue. Alcoholism had a vice grip upon my values, my mind, my body and my soul. At 19 years old I was no longer my own.

What followed was a near continuous series of blackouts, lost jobs, blaming and self-determination to overcome all of the madness. I made numerous promises to stop or control my drinking. This went on for another year before my wife became pregnant. This news instilled in me an unaccustomed optimism and a renewed determination to be a better man. I joined the army in an effort to provide provision for my soon-to-be-growing family, as well as a sense of masculinity and purpose to my own life.

After some explaining, the army took me as a private, E-2 (I had some college credit), with the prospect of gaining technical training in the field of telecommunications. A six-week stint at boot camp provided my longest period of abstinence (not sobriety—a term I will later define) and illustrated some of my leadership characteristics. I felt confident and finally finished something I had set out to accomplish—graduating from boot camp and preparing for our move to advanced training school. My first son was born three days before my graduation, so I wasn't allowed to leave the post. However, I was soon home for a ten-day leave and experienced for the first time the joy of fatherhood. I cradled my newborn son in my arms and fed him in the early morning hours. This was, and still remains in retrospect some 30 years later, an experience of awe and unconditional—almost unfathomable—love. For this brief time I enjoyed a reprieve from all my fears and failures; all of the insanity seemed distant. I truly believed during this respite that I could be a good husband and father after all. These were the deepest desires of my heart, and I felt vital and authentic.

My leave ended and I departed for Augusta, Georgia, to begin a six-month training program with the Army Signal Corps. I was drunk when I arrived at the base—late for my platoon assignment. This would define my strategy for the duration of my training experience. I nearly got kicked out but managed to squeak past the closing ranks and observations of my supervisors. An assignment to Fort Stewart, Georgia, facilitated my rapid departure, under the auspices of official transfer orders.

My second son was born in April 1984 in Savannah, Georgia. I was there for his birth but quickly ducked out to celebrate with my friends back in Charleston. Two days later I returned back to the hospital in time to pick up my wife and newborn son. Her parents (my in-laws) were furious, and I was deeply embarrassed and ashamed. This had become old habit long before that point.

To complicate matters, the US Army responds differently to absences than does, say, Pizza Hut. I quickly discovered that my ability to manipulate through shallow excuses was limited. Being absent from an assigned position isn't an inconvenience in the military; it can equate to the difference between life and death. How the situation goes in peacetime and base assignment predicts how things will go on the battlefield. Failure to attend to one's responsibilities can kill a fellow soldier. And the powers that be treat it that way.

Fortunately, my first official offense in AWOL (absent without leave) resulted in a sanction known as an Article 13. This entails forfeited pay, loss of rank and the addition of extra work assignments. They should have shot me; my wife would have congratulated them for the effort. Instead I met this consequence with the same victim stance and defiance I had demonstrated at the time of my DUI charge. My problems were always someone—or everyone—else's fault.

I left the following weekend in quest of consolation with my friends back in Charleston. Upon my drunken return to Savannah, I abruptly remembered that it was my older son's birthday. I ducked into the local mall to procure a gift before proceeding home. When I "came to" (remember the blackouts?), I was standing in my apartment, holding a garden hose and some Easter egg bubble gum and wondering how in the hell I had gotten here. My wife's screaming made it more difficult to comprehend the situation, but when she left with the kids I simply enjoyed the solitude of self-pity.

Author's note: *Remember in the forward (you read it, right?) that I said this gets ugly? At this point in the story it would appear that it already has. Unfortunately, there's more. But stay with me on—or should I say* through—*this; it does get better. Of course, I had no reason at the time to recognize this.*

When I ran off to visit friends I almost always had some involvement with my oldest brother. At 15 years my elder he unwittingly played multiple roles in my life—brother, friend and father figure. Bill and I always connected at a deep and mutual level of love and respect. He was and remains an intimate friend. He also struggled with addiction—his own demons harking, at least in part, back to atrocities experienced during his teenage years fighting to survive in the battlefields and swamps of Vietnam.

If we've lived long enough, each one of us has had something stolen from us. Too often this seems to be some aspect of innocence. I often feel as though a lot of what we pursue through addiction is a return to the natural state for which we were created—guilelessness, safety and love. If even for a brief moment we could taste the essence of that original state, the experience would change us forever. Some of us live passionately—and desperately—enough to chase this euphoria in the hope of catching some fleeting glimpse. Many alcoholics are like that—incessantly running either toward or away from something.

Bill was arrested in 1984 for a felony and is now serving a life sentence. I felt as though he had died, that yet another piece of my life had been wrested from me. Alone again.

To pound the proverbial nail in my military/vocational coffin, I was arrested for a second DUI in Savannah. The army stripped me of my security clearance and busted me in rank to buck private. They also confined me to quarters when I wasn't working and sent me for counseling. It was here that I was first introduced to Alcoholics Anonymous. I was madder than hell, looking desperately for a way out.

This led to an impulsive abandonment of both my family and the military. I just left—walked away. In a brief communication to my wife I directed her to pack it all up and go home to her parents. I was going to disappear for a while, find work somewhere and somehow just start over. She had no fight left in her—mostly glad to go home and leave me to my nonsense.

This went on for a year or so. I eventually turned myself in at an army base and was discharged under less than honorable conditions, for the good of the service. They didn't want to waste a bullet or a brig cell on me. Alcoholics will do that to the people with whom they associate—suck the life out of them until they're exhausted and apathetic—resigned, eager to just find some time and space away from the problem drinker. A useful survival skill.

Reflection Questions

Sometimes we make choices to do things that are irrational, self-destructive and/or self-defeating. Even with good intention.

1. Identify two examples of times when you did something with good intention, only to have it backfire (or bring about unintended consequences)?
2. Are our "good" intentions enough to justify bad behavior? Why or why not?
3. Do you believe that what you do with your life is your own business? Elaborate beyond a yes or no.
4. Should we consider other people's welfare when making decisions with regard to our lives? Why or why not?

6

DENIAL AND ALCOHOLISM EXPLAINED

Now I'm steppin' into the twilight zone.
The place is a madhouse,
Feels like being cloned.
My beacon's been moved
Under moon and star.
Where am I to go
Now that I've gone too far?
Soon you will come to know
When the bullet hits the bone.

—Golden Earring, "Twilight Zone," 1982

Withdrawal symptoms from alcohol overuse include headache, tremors, hallucinations, anxiety, heart palpitations, seizures and even death from cardiac arrest. Withdrawal from alcohol, as well as central nervous system depressants, can be fatal if the user has acquired significant tolerance. Extensive quantity and frequency of use escalate the issue. Binge drinkers are highly susceptible to these symptoms because of the prolonged and extensive intake of the psychoactive substance.

My patterns of drinking had begun to take shape. Acutely aware at this point that I had a problem, I tried to control my drinking. This included drinking beer only, drinking only on certain days, avoiding hard spirits and avoiding certain people and places.

Another aspect of alcoholism is denial. The mind must make sense of the insanity that emanates from addictive behavior. Abrupt changes in sense of identity, determination and choice, followed by bizarre actions when under the influence, serve to confound the individual's best efforts to resolve the problem of drinking. Blackouts add to the confusion, along with intense guilt and remorse. It's a dreadful predicament not to be able to predict one's own choices or actions. The person has no sense of internal control and feels as though they are susceptible to any random thought, impulse or idea. In a real sense this is actually true. It seems as though they might even lose their mind. Many do.

According to long established research, a problem drinker or drug user will go through several phases of development (see detail to follow) before coming to full acceptance of their problem. Without successful completion of these phases, there is no hope of recovery. Addiction is a progressive disease, continuously gaining ground in terms of its deterioration of the human will. It refuses to relent and takes on a life of its own. Many never complete the process of gaining insight and remain stuck, eventually dying or going insane. Others experience breakthrough, but only after a prolonged period of trial and error.

According to Terrence Gorski, author of *Staying Sober—A Guide to Relapse Prevention*, there are five stages an addicted person will pass through to reach full acceptance of their condition.

These necessary steps are key to motivational readiness—a sincere and engrained desire to pursue an entire lifestyle change through a bona fide and formal process of recovery. Gorski's book is an excellent resource for gaining insight into the personality and nature of the addicted person. These attitudes are manifested in a thought pattern that goes something like this:

When confronted with the idea that they have a problem with their alcohol/drug use, the person responds with:

1. "I don't have a problem; *you* have a problem," implying that all is well in my life and that you should mind your own business. This is a full denial of all problems and a disconnect from reality.

2. "Okay, I have problems, but they aren't related to my alcohol/drug use." This is a slight break in denial, at least in terms of admitting the presence of life problems. Notice that the denial still holds up with regard to the aspect of substance use. Don't expect any obvious behavioral changes at this stage.

3. "Okay, I have problems, and they may be related to alcohol/drug use." At this point the individual is experiencing a greater degree of dissolution of their denial paradigm. In this phase the user will attempt to control their consumption of psychoactive substances. They aren't ready to quit but are beginning to recognize and accept that there is a problem.

4. "Okay, I can't control my use. I'll just quit." This stated intention is indicative of a greater breakdown in the denial system. . . but don't get your hopes up yet. The addict/alcoholic is exercising willpower and determination but is unwilling to seek genuine help. There is no internal commitment to face and work at

changing deep personality issues. The individual will not at this juncture usually seek treatment, twelve-step support groups, changes in lifestyle, etc. The intention is to keep on living the way they have, but just not drinking.

5. "Oh my God, I *am* one [an alcoholic/addict]!" When these former steps fail (and they will), at long last a realization, an act of revelation and grace, falls upon the mind and heart of the addict. Acknowledgment of failure and the full implications of alcoholism/addiction drop into the thought process like an uninvited uncle on Thanksgiving Day. This realization is disruptive and overwhelming. Bill Wilson of Alcoholics Anonymous describes it this way: "He cannot picture life without alcohol. Someday he will be unable to imagine life either with alcohol or without it. He will be at the jumping off place. He will wish for the end." (*Alcoholics Anonymous*, page 152)

With my third DUI and a rehab stint already under my belt, I could and did claim that I was alcoholic. In fact, I used this as a middle-ground approach. When pressed against consequences, I would resort to playing victim and confess to my alcoholism. This ploy could suffice, on occasion, to bring some sympathy and perhaps even evoke compassion. The claim was even followed on my part by some sincere (to the degree that my distorted motives could be sincere) efforts at rehabilitation. I approached clergy, church parishioners and mental health professionals and even attended some AA meetings to try to relieve the burden. Consistency was my weak point, though, and I quickly succumbed to my incessant craving for escape. My longest period of sobriety at this point was 89 days. After that my drinking just became sporadic again—a few days or a week of abstinence here or there. Ultimately, I just quit quitting.

Reflection Questions

This is a professional discussion using nontechnical language surrounding the driving components behind addiction.
1. Have you, or someone you know, experienced an addiction problem?
2. Were you or they aware of the problem?
3. What did you or they try to do about it?
4. Do you believe that self-discipline is a solution to addiction problems? If yes, how so? If not, then why not?

Application Exercise

Attend an "open" twelve-step meeting in your area. A quick search on the web or newspaper will give some direction on the where and when. Visitors are welcome at "open" meetings.

What did you learn about the people who attend these meetings?

7

PROGRESSION OF ADDICTION AND MORAL CULPABILITY

In the shuffling madness
Of the locomotive breath,
Runs the all-time loser,
Headlong to his death.
He feels the piston scraping—
Steam breaking on his brow—
Old Charlie stole the handle and
The train won't stop going—
No way to slow down.

—Jethro Tull, "Locomotive Breath," 1971

I am the father both of two children who don't know my life and of two (more to follow on this) who never knew life. This defining statement illustrates the deprivation and loss addiction will eventually overlay upon a life that is slowly and steadily deteriorating under its influence. Addiction is a regression from all that is good, from all moral value and purpose. Every facet of life is marred, inevitably altered and distorted, perverted. The soul evolves from transparent resiliency into a grayish, static muck. Nothing really changes; life only gets darker, worse. Quicksand. The more effort expended, the deeper one is drawn into . . . what? Cold, lonely, terrifying darkness. Death, . . . but not yet, not before the torment seeps into every crevice of the mind—tainting and staining the soul. Like a leech it slowly but systematically sips life and saps light from the heart, replacing hope with a creeping despair. The nastiness that grows from this putrid organic matter only serves to perpetuate the regression. Cynicism, fear, terror. A brute force survival instinct replaces any sense of love or concern for others. Bondage and slavery are engrained—this master will share with no other. Alcohol or [pick your idol . . .] demands full allegiance and encases the will in order to ensure this loyalty.

Relational emptiness and isolation framed my existence. In my ongoing circle of dysfunctional relationships, I encountered a lonely and adventurous housewife. We met at a bar and spent the next six months plying and pillaging the forbidden garden of infidelity. I was a thief and a liar by nature—no excuses now. The coming scenes from this chapter encompass both comedic and tragic narrative. Comedic as in my running through the backyards of neighbors, half dressed, tripping over dogs and getting caught on fences, all in pursuit of a quick exit after an unexpected return home by her husband.

Tragic as in another unplanned pregnancy and resulting abortion. So I can once again add murderer to my descriptive list of moral characteristics. After which, again, I was dumped—another rejection to add to my portfolio.

Let's step out of this story for a moment and address two terms: *unplanned* and *another*.

How is it that we experience *unplanned* events like auto accidents or pregnancies? I'm not talking here about those seemingly random and genuinely unforeseen events that punctuate every life, the pure accidents. No, my reference is to avoidable exigencies in life, whether or not we're willing to acknowledge that fact—those negative situations and outcomes our indiscretions play right in to. Was that pregnancy really unplanned, beyond the sphere of my control? How about that car accident? Or was I just somehow hoping the odds were against this happening to me? One can avoid pregnancy by abstaining from sex; any course of action beyond abstinence is playing with risk and probability. While the pregnancy may not have been planned in terms of this being the anticipated or sought after consequence, I must admit that I knew the risks and did what I damn well wanted to do anyway, hoping things would turn out differently. Even ignorance, had that to some small degree been a factor (perhaps my partner was lying about her own protection), wouldn't have gotten me off the hook. If I don't know the risk relative to a given behavior, I have to make a conscious decision to consider the deficit in knowledge and then decide whether to evaluate the risks or disregard them. Same culpability.

Same scenario with a vehicular accident. "She was driving along the interstate and lost control of the vehicle when the car in front of her suddenly stopped" may be construed as "she was driving too close to the car in front of her." There's a well-known rule of thumb to this: maintain one additional car length's distance for every additional 10 miles per hour in speed. Anything compromised in the math increases the risk factor and probability of a mishap. The resulting crash isn't an accident but the result of carelessness.

Okay, how about the word *another,* as in implying *"again?"* Humans have the ability to apply prior lessons from experience and project the learning forward. We're endowed with an abstract ability to visualize, or predict an outcome—or at least a possible outcome—to a future choice. To do this one must be willing to assimilate past experiences in the light of their true implications and exercise integrity in the moment of decision to apply this knowledge. For example:

"When I've worn socks on the slippery stairwell, I've slipped and fallen down the stairs."

Lesson: Either don't wear socks on the stairwell or be extra cautious (risk reduction) and use the railing when descending the stairwell in those socks you insist on wearing.

If I disregard this lesson, the next time I walk down the stairwell I face a calculated risk of falling again. This is because:
1. Gravity still holds sway.
2. Friction even more so.
3. My socks are still slippery.
4. I *will* fall again—if not now, then some other time.

So, if I fall down *another* time, who is responsible for this tragic event? Now let's expand this beyond socks and stairs: If I continually experience rejection in relationships, could it be that *I'm* either choosing poor relational partners or failing to relate effectively? In the never-ending blame game so favored in my culture, I can perpetually be—or claim to be—a victim of other people's thoughtless actions. When I choose to live out of that paradigm, I'm doomed to continue along the path of *another's* choices, consequences and behaviors. So when I make reference to yet *another* rejection, *another* abandonment or *another* repetition of whatever sort, I'm telling you that I haven't taken the responsibility to make different choices about the who, how or where of my own life's journey. Self-fulfilling prophecy and all that. This stuff perpetuates itself.

The decimation of my heart continued, and I continued to seek answers outside the scope of my drinking. Alcoholics Anonymous was always a welcome respite, but I couldn't make my home there. Not yet. Ditto the church. Every tentative turn only continued to arc along my accustomed circle of futility. My life at this point was characterized by numerous job changes—I equated six months with longevity—and living wherever I could for as long as I could. I can't tell you how many couches served as my personal space / sleeping quarters.

I had occasional visits with my children and ex-wife. She had finally filed for divorce under the habitual drunkenness provision, allowing for a quick exit under family court law. I was served and arrived at Family Court for the hearing, making no pretense of a fight. She had brought several witnesses in anticipation of my defense, but their input wasn't needed. One after another these friends reluctantly testified of my drunken escapades, recounting in intricate detail things that had either never happened or that I had somehow managed to forget—if I'd even been aware of them at the time. I didn't mind. I was more or less numb—wanting the ordeal to be over while at the same time hoping some miraculous breakthrough might come of it.

What did come from it was a court order for child support, and rightly so. This would prove to be another barometer of my failure as both father and provider. Over the course of the next five years I fell continually behind in these payments and was incarcerated on this basis numerous times. I once heard a fellow say that you can do a life sentence in the county jail 30 days at a time. I now know what he meant—I was a frequent flier in the Charleston County Jail for both child support and DUI.

I was a failure at two of the most important roles a man can know—those of father and husband. Alcohol took possession of my soul and, with it, the deepest treasures of my heart. I would go on to lose my parental rights as a father through adoption—a choice to which I conceded so that my ex-wife could move on with her life. While I had hopes and a vague agreement that I could see them again, this never materialized. I have not seen my biological children since 1988, despite numerous attempts to reach out to them. This is a loss that has haunted my waking moments for decades.

I earned that fifth DUI in 1986, passing through Moncks Corner, South Carolina, at around 3:00 a.m. I was involved in an all-nighter in a borrowed car, looking for more beer and weaving precariously between streetlights and mailboxes.

Computer databases and DUI sentencing in the mid 1980s weren't what they are today, so when I was charged with a third instead of a fifth DUI I felt as though I'd been living on bonus points. I convinced my mother to post the $500 bond and was released after a week. Another wakeup call to stop drinking, . . . and I was once again determined to try.

I enrolled in some outpatient counseling and returned to AA. More insights and more effort, for sure. I even began to feel better, got to know some recovering people and connected. I was still hedging some, only going to a few meetings per week. Most recovering folks recommend attending 90 meetings within 90 days, but at this stage I still felt as though this was not only a bit excessive but inconvenient.

As was my pattern, though, I couldn't live within my own skin. Hounded by a pervasive sense of anxiety and loneliness, I caved to the obsession for a drink, defenseless as always when this intense urge took hold of me. Most of my efforts up to this point amounted to attempts to keep the urge from arising. Somehow, when it did emerge (and it invariably does in early recovery), my defenses were totally ineffective.

There's a pattern to this problem of craving and obsession:

The first thing that happens, at least in my awareness, is an agitation or annoyance of sorts, followed by a lack of motivation or a sense of apathy. Sometimes I was aware of what was happening and would mentally resist it. It's precisely at this point that I inevitably fell short. The next prescribed step—all I had to do at that point—was to call someone else in recovery. This sharing of the burden is critical; it's a reaching outside one's personal limitations to enter the community of intimate need and fellowship. But I either couldn't or wouldn't follow through.

For reasons I couldn't have explained at the time but understand better now, I was immobilized when it came to reaching out. From that point I would experience a rapid "wear down" of my mental defenses, and the obsession would overrun me. I would formulate an argument or justification for breaking away from whatever was holding me in the recovery orbit and find myself thrust into the gravitational pull of yet another—big time—drinking binge.

This stuck point would cycle over and over again for several more years. Failure to overcome this hurdle would perpetuate my continual downward trajectory—I was hurtling toward the grave, although not yet. By the grace of God I was to live long enough to see through the dilemma. Long enough to perceive the shame and guilt, embedded in early childhood experiences and reinforced in a life of bad choices and addiction. Long enough to recognize the life compressed under spiritual assault and deprived of the "beloved son" relationship with God to which repentance and acceptance of Christ's atoning sacrifice "entitled" me. More on this later . . .

By this time my binges had taken on a pattern all their own. In terms of my consumption patterns, a day of drinking equated to drinking all day, not eating (or eating very little) until passing out, and starting the next day with a drink, . . . only to continue on with the cycle.

If I drank for fewer than three days I could stop when I wanted. But if I entered a fourth consecutive day of drinking I would experience withdrawal symptoms that had to be managed. Most of the time I could "wean" myself off the drink and suffer through the consequences. Sometimes, though, this situation led to admission to a detoxification center. The phrase "I need a drink" isn't necessarily an exaggeration for an alcoholic. Oftentimes he/she is aware of the body's reaction to withdrawal and has more than once experienced the severe and debilitating pain of withdrawal. Enduring this phase now becomes essential to functioning.

Another rendezvous in the bar crowd led to another significant relationship. I lived with Rhonda, in fact, for almost five years. The relationship started badly and grew continually worse. As a buddy of mine in AA recounts in terms of his own story, "We took turns beating each other up and calling the cops on each other." This was more accurate in my own case than I would like to admit. The push-pull of codependency and alcoholism created a mesmerizing tension that, ironically, bonded us together and from which neither of us could pull away. Move in, move out, invited in, thrown out—a love-hate cycle of hostage negotiations. She drank in the same way I did, so neither of us was able to take charge.

In her defense I need to clarify that none of my drinking or dysfunction was in any way her responsibility. She had a good heart and, like most of us in survival mode, was living out of a deeply wounded soul. But there was no way either of us could have survived this relationship long term.

In all fairness she did support some of my efforts to quit drinking. Counseling and AA were cycling around for me on a regular basis now, at least two to three times per year. Slowly I was working out of the addiction fog and pressing into a change of life, though I had absolutely no clue what this change would ultimately look like. In retrospect I can see the persistent hand of God steadying my walk toward the place where He could finally reach and rescue me. If I had been able to rationally assess the situation at this point, I would have conceded that there were overwhelming odds against any type of redemption. Staying alive constituted a miracle in itself. In reality, though, this very cycle marked the patient and determined pursuit of God to reclaim my life.

Reflection Questions

This chapter has provided (1) illustrations of the moral deterioration related to a life entrapped by addiction; (2) a picture of compromised values and the decimation of the soul; (3) philosophical commentary on free will, moral choice, decisions and personal responsibility; (4) a depiction of the rapid progression of alcoholism to its late stage; and (5) the near inevitability of divorce.

1. In his discussion of "unplanned" events, the author raises the possibility that some "accidents" are really the direct and predictable results of reckless or careless behaviors. What is your take on this issue?
2. Are there now, or have there been dysfunctional patterns of choices in your life where you have refused to look realistically at your role in the process? Have your problems and setbacks always been "someone else's" fault? This concept could extend beyond relationships to spending, employment or even church life.
3. Are you a victim of other people's choices? Explain your response one way or the other.

8

HOPE WITHIN THE STORM

... I am the sweat from Your brow
But You love me anyway
I am the nail in Your wrist
But You love me anyway
I am Judas' kiss
But You love me anyway
See now, I am the man that called out from the crowd
For Your blood to be spilled on this earth shaking ground
Yes then, I turned away with this smile on my face
With this sin in my heart tried to bury Your grace
And then alone in the night, I still called out for You
So ashamed of my life, my life, my life ...
But You love me anyway
Oh, God how you love me
You love me anyway
It's like nothing in life that I've ever known
You love me anyway
Oh Lord, how You love me.

—Sidewalk Prophets, *"You Love Me Anyway"*

God works that way sometimes. The odds seem to stack against us. Life ebbs away and we spiral into cavernous depths we could only describe as hell on earth. We see ourselves as maimed, scarred, and repulsive. We spit back like wild animals, insisting on our own will and self-sufficiency—like apathetic, cornered rats against the onslaught of an overwhelming predator. We fight against the graces of God and blame *Him* for our condition. At least we accuse Him of indifference, all the while looking beyond and away to another lover to provide the comfort we so desperately crave.

John Wesley, an eighteenth-century theologian and founder of the movement called Methodism, states that the downfall of humanity wasn't pride. That belonged to the devil. Instead, he says, we collectively fell into the chasm of distrust. We believe Satan's lies and feel as though God is holding out on us, that we need to make do for ourselves. Self-sufficiency breeds contempt, self-centeredness and an alienation from the One who loves us and longs to care for our hearts. For now and for eternity.

Some of my vaunted self-sufficiency was beginning to crumble. As I referenced in the earlier chapter regarding motivational readiness, I started to believe "I *am* one! [an alcoholic]" Willingness and honesty were within my grasp. But I couldn't grab them . . . yet.

On one of those "thrown out" or "walked out" events of my most recent courtship, I left Charleston in a beat-up '72 Chrysler—something I had managed to pick up along one of my more stable life cycles (that two-month window). Honestly, one could play a doubles set of tennis on the hood of this car, it was so large. The steering had about four yards of "play," meaning you had to keep turning the wheel drastically left and right to keep it centered on the road. You could be stark raving sober and look like a habitual drunk, navigating between mailboxes and trashcans. It would have been easier to throw an anchor out the window to slow the car down than to rely on the paper-thin metal that served as brake pads. You had to time your stops. All of this assuming you could get the damn thing started. This proposition entailed a combination of prayer and cussing, and once it fired up you had to determine the benefit of keeping it running for several hours against the inevitable delay of waking it up again.

It was in this rectangular death trap (did I mention it was sort of a "booger" green?) that I left Charleston at around 5:00 one morning. After a night of drinking and no sleep, I had designed my escape plan and pointed my life and vehicle in the general direction of Florida. I don't recall for sure, but I think I was going to drop in on one of my siblings with a grand plan of couch surfing for a while. Everyone likes it when one of these relatives drops in for a visit.

I stocked up on beer and cigarettes—the essential provisions of any reputable drunk, gassed up (yep—left the car running) and started down US Highway 17 South. I remember arriving on the south side of Savannah, Georgia, and pulling in to a diner to gather my wits. I knew I was too intoxicated to keep this up and, I guess, must have dozed off for a while (car still running). I resumed the journey and somewhere along I-95 south, near Brunswick, Georgia, was pulled over by a state trooper. Thank God.

I was about to set a new career record.

Blood alcohol level (BAL) is a unit of measurement that can be used to determine the level of impairment of a motor vehicle operator. This is measured within a decimal system and establishes a threshold for legal status. For example, as of this writing, the legal limit for a BAL in South Carolina is .08. That 0 in front of the 8 is important. Anything over a .1 is gaining significantly in severity as it relates to impairment.

There are variables that affect the BAL. Women absorb alcohol at faster rates than men. Body weight is inversely proportional to the effects of alcohol—the more weight, the more alcohol it takes to raise the BAL. Finally, food intake, medications, health issues and metabolism contribute to the level of alcohol in the bloodstream. Below is a chart to illustrate.

Blood Alcohol Level Chart
Progressive effects of alcohol:

BAC (% by vol.)	Behavior	Impairment
0.010–0.029	• Average individual appears normal • Mild euphoria • Relaxation	• Subtle effects that can be detected with special tests
0.030–0.059	• Joyousness • Talkativeness • Decreased inhibition	• Concentration
0.06–0.09	• Blunted feelings • Disinhibition • Extroversion	• Reasoning • Depth perception • Peripheral vision • Glare recovery
0.10–0.19	• Over-expression • Emotional swings • Anger or sadness • Boisterousness • Decreased libido	• Reflexes • Reaction time • Gross motor control • Staggering • Slurred speech • Temporary erectile dysfunction • Possibility of temporary alcohol poisoning

0.20–0.29	• Stupor • Loss of understanding • Impaired sensations • Possibility of falling unconscious	• Severe motor impairment • Loss of consciousness • Memory blackout
0.30–0.39	• Severe central nervous system depression • Unconsciousness • Possibility of death	• Bladder function • Breathing • Disequilibrium
0.40–0.50	• General lack of behavior • Unconsciousness • Possibility of death	• Breathing • Heart rate • Positional Alcohol Nystagmus
>0.50	• High risk of poisoning/death	

(Source: http://en.wikipedia.org/wiki/Blood_alcohol_content)

I was rarely a belligerent drunk, at least not when the party I faced was holding a gun. When caught I usually cooperated with the authorities. I spoke and interacted with the trooper and cooperatively went through the field sobriety test. I easily recall this as I write it.

When I was booked into the Glynn County jail that afternoon, my BAL was registered at .36. The chart above references this category as severe, with the possibility of death, unconsciousness and severe central nervous system depression (the nervous system manages heart rate, breathing and metabolism). I mention this to denote my level of tolerance to the effects of alcohol and my ability to consume exorbitant quantities. This is an indicator of late- stage alcoholism. Such was my case at the age of 26.

I made bail and later skipped out on this charge. Again, lack of technology played into my ability to do this. I was charged with first offense DUI, but by my count this was number six.

Some of my readers may take offense at what may come off as levity on my part in the face of this lack of justice. Please hear me: I take no pride in this recollection. I could easily have killed someone and am truly grateful this didn't happen. This was more than an example of irresponsibility; it was gross negligence and a total disregard for human life on my part. I see it for what it was and offer no rationale for why I escaped the potentially severe consequences of my actions. I can truthfully say that my life lessons with regard to my active alcoholism have since been applied; I have worked diligently both to help prevent this from happening with others and to keep it in the forefront of my own mind.

Like the notorious parolee in *Les Misérables* who encounters mercy at the hands of a Bishop, I cling to the love and forgiveness of a benevolent and merciful God. In the scene I have in mind, the scandalous character Jean Valjean has been apprehended and returned to the victim of his recent burglary. Rather than participating in the judgment, the Bishop directs the intervention to appear as a misunderstanding to his captors, who leave the two alone in a tense encounter in the garden. This is a remarkable example of mercy displacing justice through a catalyst of love. Jean Valjean is speechless as the Bishop grabs him by the collar and states:

> "Now Don't Forget, Don't ever Forget, you've promised to become a new man."
>
> "Promise? What? Why are you doing this?"

> "Jean Valjean, my brother, you no longer belong to evil. With this silver, I have bought your soul. I've ransomed you from fear and hatred, and now I give you back to God."
>
> —Victor Hugo, *Les Misérables*, 1862

On September 21–22 Hurricane Hugo slammed into Charleston with an unprecedented force in modern history. While the area is no stranger to hurricanes and tropical storms, many people had grown passive regarding evacuations. Preparedness was often a haphazard gathering of perishable foods and perhaps a dramatic show of action, like nailing plywood over windows. It had been many years since a significant storm had damaged the low country. Apathy and indifference had replaced diligence. For the most part, the general consensus was "It won't happen here, or at least not this time."

I actually welcomed the storm for its promise of chaos and distraction—a diversion from the increasing scrutiny and consequences of my lifestyle. I had violated probation in a number of ways and was significantly behind in child support. People were looking for me, and without good intention.

I had just lost another job and was engaged in my own preparation for the storm. Picking up the meager paycheck and as much beer as I could afford, I hunkered down in my shared home with friends to ride out the storm. Somewhere between the passage of the hurricane's eye and the storm's end I passed out. I recall waking to a numbing silence except for the sound of running water outside. It was as dark as I had ever seen. A large tree had been uprooted in the front yard and ripped out the water meter with it. The next month's bill would arrive for the use and disposal of 44,000 gallons of water. For once in my life I had a legitimate explanation.

The devastation the hurricane caused created a cloud of confusion behind which I could, and did, hide for months. Work was readily available for the laborer, and my checkered and unreliable past was obscured. Law enforcement and family court were occupied with many more pressing matters, so I was immune from their worrisome influence.

Reflection Questions

This chapter contains a theological discussion on God's sovereignty/grace and the alienation and rebellion of humankind.

1. If God were sitting next to you, just having a cola and shooting the breeze, what two questions would you ask Him?
2. What have been some of your assumptions about God's attitude toward you? Has He:
    a. been distant or indifferent?
    b. been holding out on you, being unfair?
    c. been disappointed in you?
    d. been attentive, kind, pursuing and loving.
3. What did you think about the dialogue from the movie clip from *Les Misérables*?
    a. Do you believe that God looks at your life with compassion, love and forgiveness?
    b. What would keep you from believing, or has kept you from believing, that this is true?

Application Exercise

Take 10 minutes each day, for five consecutive days, to sit in silence, if possible where you can be completely undisturbed. Ask God, "Do you love me like that?" or "How do you see me?" Repeat the question several times, slowly and out loud. Listen in your mind for an answer. See whether you sense or hear anything. Write it down. Is there someone you can trust with whom you can share God's answer?

9

BREAKDOWN ... OR BREAKTHROUGH?

I was waiting for the day you'd come around.
I was chasing, but nothing was all I found.
From the moment you came into my life,
You showed me what's right.

And it feels like tonight,
I can't believe I'm broken inside.
Can't you see that there's nothing that I wanna do,
But try to make it up to you?
And it feels like tonight,
Tonight.

—Excerpt from Chris Daughtry, *"Feels Like Tonight,"* 2008

Over the course of the next 18 months I would continue the cycle of binge drinking and recovery. Brief periods of reprieve were always followed by relapse. I re-entered my twelve-step support group in September 1990. There was something different about this time. In hindsight, I can see that I approached and engaged in a different manner. One distinction was that I started getting to know people in attendance. Beyond a passing greeting or a polite "Everything's fine," I started to spend time with a group of about eight to ten peers. We were all about the same age and shared many commonalities. Our compatible stories, addiction consequences and struggles were also similar. This provided proximity to positive peers, as well as identification with others. When this occurs it significantly reduces the stress and guilt that accompany multiple life failures. I started to believe that I did belong somewhere and that I might be able to do this thing; more significantly, I *wanted* to succeed.

I relapsed five times within six months from September 1990 through April 7, 1991. With each relapse I felt as though I were drifting further and further away from the opportunity to recover. Whereas earlier I had rationalized my relapses as just changing my mind, I was now fearfully aware that I might not have the capacity to get sober. I had seen many people die from this, and many more being incarcerated. I quickly returned to my recovery group each time and pressed in more and more intensely: more tears, more desperation, more commitment, more determination.

A psychological study has revealed how commitment can be ingrained and cultivated. Using the concept of initiation into college fraternities, social scientists discovered that a correlation exists between how much someone will endure in order to obtain a desired goal or object and their level of commitment to keep it. The more endurance required to overcome obstacles, the more deeply commitment is formed and ingrained. Once that commitment is acquired, the victor maintains a metaphorical grip that is nearly unbreakable. Without this sacrifice, accomplishments or acquirements lose their value and commitment wanes, resulting in loss through neglect or indifference. For the acquisition of sobriety, this principle is critical.

In early 1991 I enrolled in an evening Intensive Outpatient Program—another attempt to find freedom. The format of this type of treatment offers both intensity and flexibility. Meeting three evenings a week a person can hold down (or try) employment while devoting considerable effort to addressing the addiction problem. This is supplemented with individual and family counseling. The addict is also required to engage in twelve-step support group meetings. All in all, it's affordable and effective treatment.

I gained some traction and learned more about the bio-psycho-social-spiritual nature of my disease. Relational dynamics and relapse prevention skills were also incorporated. I was being equipped. I was learning. The fog was lifting.

I remember most of the events leading up to March 21, 1990, the day that started my last relapse. I was working full time, attending my counseling sessions, attending twelve-step meetings and doing the homework. I was home from work that day because of rain and was moving about some altered routine. Opening the refrigerator door I passed my hand over the twelve-pack of beer to get something to eat. My eyes locked in on this, and I quickly shut the door, . . . opened it again and re-shut it, . . . opened it again . . . Unbelievable as it sounds, this went on for an hour. I would walk out of the room and back in, repeating the fatal ritual that was relentlessly and seductively pulling my heart back toward the idol.

I had the vague notion I should call someone about this. Had I exercised that proposition, my sobriety date to this very day would have been different. But I didn't. My thought processes were clouded with the obsession to get drunk. Honestly, the reason I didn't call was that I had already decided to drink. The resistance at this point was the smaller part of my will. I knew that if I did call a friend in recovery they would likely succeed in talking me out of my intention. By the time I became consciously aware of the intervention needed in order to preserve my sobriety my addictive thinking had already taken over. The "bad guy" had taken the bullets out of the gun, and I found myself totally defenseless.

The next three weeks were horrific: round-the-clock drinking, night terrors, shakes, tremors—followed up by the need for a drink to ward off withdrawals. I finally hit the wall on April 7, 1991, awakening at a friend's house on that warm spring morning.

I knew what I had to do. With enough clarity to make a phone call I contacted the local detox unit and obtained permission to be screened for admission. I drank two beers, caught a ride back home (where I had left my clothes) and persuaded my girlfriend to give me a ride to the facility. At around 11:00 a.m. she left me in the parking lot with $1.50 in cigarette money and the last two swigs of a hot beer. I tossed this back and walked up the stairs of the aging building. I heard a voice inside me with the ominous reminder "Every time you drink this will happen." My heart response was "I get it."

I spent three days in the unit. My vital signs were alarming, and I was fortunate to rebound as quickly as I did. My sponsor picked me up and I went immediately to a recovery meeting. Even though I had continually relapsed, my friends welcomed me back with a genuine love that soothed my aching heart. I felt overwhelming gratitude to be sitting with them, unaffected by shaking or sickness. Instead I was overcome by the realization of my renewed ability to taste life. Something unique was taking over. I felt like a man set free from death row. Free and alive!

Reflection Questions

The author describes his entry into sustained recovery from alcoholism.

1. Have you attempted to make a lifestyle change or some improvement in your life without experiencing long-term success?
2. How much of our success should depend on our own discipline and how much on our reliance upon God? Is there some level of cooperation involved in this? How not or how so?

10

EMERGING FROM DARKNESS

"The pupil dilates in darkness and in the end finds light, just as the soul dilates in misfortune and in the end finds God."

—Victor Hugo, *Les Misérables*, 1862

The Developmental Model of Recovery (Gorski-Miller, 1986) serves as a road map to define and illustrate the process by which addicted people move toward full restoration. As alcoholism is a bio-psycho-social disease, these goals encompass the width and breadth of the human composition. The mind, body and soul are all adversely affected by addiction, so the recovery process must restore life in each of these domains.

There are six stages to this process. I will also include the corresponding timelines in which these are typically accomplished:

- Transition/Pretreatment: Precedes awareness of a problem. Timeline is indefinite.
- Stabilization: 6–18 Months
- Early: 1–3 Years
- Middle: 3–6 Years

- Late: 6–9 Years
- Maintenance: 10+ years

Every stage corresponds to a set of goals that are critical to addressing the deficit and the restoration of the recovering person's quality of life. Failure to confront and resolve these goals creates a "crack"—an incompleteness in the recovery foundation. Some buildings are more stable than others due to their construction characteristics and firm foundations. The strength or quality of life of a recovering person is revealed in how thorough and how well they've worked through these developmental goals.

My twelve-step support group had provided me with a fresh approach to God. I'd been a reluctant participant in this program, often struggling with the looseness that defined, or failed to define, this "Higher Power." My religiosity and self-righteousness clouded my ability to find humility. At bottom I didn't like the personal responsibility humility implied—the individual effort and ongoing work required. The 12 steps comprise an arduous task of self-inspection (and introspection), repentance and responsibility. I'd been looking for an instant miracle that would simply remove my obsession to drink. Instead I had to come to the understanding that this transition would be a lifestyle, a permanent program for living. It had already taken seven years of frequent relapses—five, as I've mentioned, in the six months just prior to these attempts—to acquire long-term sobriety.

Following my long-awaited breakthrough this new lifestyle brought me into a fully restored and fulfilled life. Spiritual development, vocational and educational pursuits, marriage and family quickly followed. It was as though someone had poured water on the proverbial seed from "Jack and the Beanstalk"—everything just "took off."

First Year

Early recovery brought many changes—beginning with some tough choices and sacrifices, which amounted to letting go of self-defeating thoughts and behaviors. Even though these lifestyle alterations were for my betterment, they often felt like painful departures.

This started with quitting my full-time job with a guy who had fired and rehired me countless times over the previous two years. My counselor's recommendation to enter a full-time, intensive outpatient program was met on my part with a frustrated obedience. I would have to attend therapy groups on Monday through Friday from 9:00 a.m.–4:00 p.m., as well as a recovery meeting once a day, seven days a week. There was no way to hold a job and do this too.

I complied with this recommendation out of a newly acquired posture of humility—a pious term for someone who has been beaten nearly to death with the weighty club of realty and is now willing to be "teachable." I hated the idea of sitting in therapy groups all day long and considered this a strong indicator of my weakness—construed as a diminishment of my masculinity. After all, real men should be working, and the absence of this activity exposed the false beliefs I had unconsciously embraced about myself.

I had made arrangements to continue to live with Rhonda and pursue treatment. I had also managed to line up some weekend work with a fellow in recovery who had a landscaping business. The bus ride to the treatment center took an hour and a half in the morning but three hours back in the evening. I'm not totally sure why that was, since the distance and route were identical. One factor was that the return trip entailed an extended delay and resulting layover, so I had plenty of time to either think or read. I chose the latter, but based on my experience that thinking could be a dangerous activity to undertake.

The six-week commitment gave me the opportunity and enforced structure to fully prioritize and apply recovery principles. There were many "triggers" (the mental activators that initiate addictive thinking) to manage throughout this time. Not surprisingly, I encountered an assortment of characters and invitations to "party"; I learned to dismiss these, though reluctantly at times.

Navigating the tumultuous relationship with Rhonda was also a lesson in assertiveness and self-preservation. I was changing and she was not. This is often the challenge when one spouse or significant other tries to break a dysfunctional cycle and the other doesn't follow suit. Their perspective is often one that says, "You have the problem, so you do something about it." Turns out the problem is beyond the scope of one person—it's systemic to the relationship. Therefore, successful recovery requires deep commitment and action to change on the part of all family members, not just the patient. Rhonda had no intention of changing anything. I would soon have to make some tough choices.

I am extremely grateful for publicly funded treatment services. There was just no way for me to afford the help I needed. I can't express my appreciation enough for the dedication and competency of the treatment team. These people were highly compassionate and effective in assisting me through the early stages of my recovery. I was able to learn and apply lessons that formed a solid foundation for my future—lessons on introspection, relationships, communication, my disease of alcoholism, and community. I was operating from deeply ingrained misconceptions about who I was. A thick layer of denial encapsulated the trauma of my childhood and the wounded state of my soul. These individuals helped smash this, exposing the truth of who I was and what I was fighting for. As this narrative was revealed a new story began to emerge.

I moved in with my sponsor shortly after completing the intensive outpatient program. Returning yet again to my former employer I reentered full-time employment, made recovery meetings everyday and continued meeting with my counselor weekly. My new friends formed the core of my social and recreational life.

By midsummer two major events would alter the trajectory of my life forever:
1. School—an increasing desire and an opportunity to further my education.
2. Meeting my best friend and future wife.

I realized that the landscaping work was not as much fun when I wasn't drinking every day. I became bored and restless. The desire to learn began to emerge, and I decided to enroll part-time at the local technical college for a diploma in landscape irrigation. This seemed to make sense, as it would provide opportunity for me to increase my salary and provide additional challenges to my vocation.

My counselor had been suggesting that I eventually look into counseling as an occupation. Vocational Rehabilitation—a social service designed to help people with disabilities find compatible employment—had given me some attention in treatment. I had taken an aptitude and vocational placement test, with results that suggested teaching, counseling and writing as potential areas for employment. The test results also correlated the amount of education needed to enter these occupations. When I saw that piece I quickly determined that landscaping was indeed where I belonged. I simply couldn't conceptualize successfully attending college for both undergraduate and graduate level studies.

While waiting in line to enroll (online access wasn't an option in those pre-internet days), I picked up a flier for the Certificate of Human Services program. This was a one-year diploma that prepared the candidate to pursue an occupation within a variety of social service roles. By the time I got to the registration line I was convinced that this was the curriculum for me. A brief follow-up with some recovery friends and my counselor confirmed that this was a good decision.

Running ideas past trusted friends and a professional is critical to making consistently wise decisions. I was accustomed to reacting based on emotion or some unconscious mandate. I rarely ever thought my decisions through, and my life reflected this willy-nilly approach. Now I was learning to ask for help and actually applying the feedback. In the end every decision was mine to make, but having the input of others has over and over again proven invaluable.

I met my future wife—and ready-made family—in and through Robin. At 31, she had entered the same twelve-step support group as I had—oblivious at the time to all that would be required in her recovery. Her alcoholism was as advanced as mine but was somewhat concealed within a dysfunctional marriage. The mother of two children, ages eighteen months and three years, she found the rooms of recovery at the point of her greatest need. When we got to know each other she was walking out the arduous tasks and goals of recovery through the 12 steps and the fellowship. We often attended the same meetings and shared service work opportunities in the same community.

I had actually met her the previous fall, and we often socialized in the same small groups of men and women. Robin was the first female friend I had ever known. All other women in my life had been for me sources for sex or validation. She was simply *one of the gang* in my eyes, although I had by no means overlooked her beauty. Her smile was contagious, and she strongly resembled several attractive celebrities of the day. She was the most pleasant person I had ever met, always, at least from my vantage point, filling a room with joy.

Given my proclivities and track record, this should have been a recipe for disaster. Still today I can't work through all of the ramifications—theological and otherwise—as to how we connected and why we were so successful. I do know that over a casual order of onion rings at a local diner she immediately changed in my perception from good friend to soul mate. We both experienced the transformation in our relationship, were equally aware of an altered and heightened state of awareness—as though some invisible intimacy switch had been thrown, melding our hearts and minds together into a vibrant and sensuous reality. I could and might write a book on just this topic.

True love has changed my life, period. The love of God is beyond anything I've ever known. And Robin's love is and has been the second most powerful change agent in my life. She is for me the human manifestation of what God is telling and showing me every day. There is healing, joy and purpose in my life. To understate the issue, I've become a better man as a result of knowing her.

Neither of us understood at the time most of what I have just verbalized, but we were both clear on our process: recovery *first* . . . and recovery *separate*. She had her program. I had mine. She had her sponsor and higher power, neither of which was us, or me. This was the course we followed, and it served us well in preventing the relapse that seemed inevitable in light of my earlier, formative relationships.

For the next year I cut grass with a second-hand push mower and attended technical school. Robin waited tables. We built our lives around the community of recovering people and pressed into the difficulties that always come with learning a new lifestyle—a life without alcohol and chaos.

One incident nearly derailed the entire plan.

At five months into recovery I had at last surpassed the constant obsession and craving that had plagued me in my earlier attempts. At 62 days of sobriety, it just lifted. There were still annoying thoughts, but nothing that compared to the powerful seduction of that earlier craving. I had more sobriety time under my belt than I'd ever before accumulated. It was a Sunday afternoon on a warm summer day, with chicken frying on the stove.

The children were a delightful assimilation into my new reality. Without overstepping my presence or authority, I had entwined myself into their lives, and a reciprocating enjoyment had begun to emerge. I enjoyed wrestling and playing with them, assembling and repairing toys, following along with chores and the like. They helped fill a void where my biological children had once resided. On this particular day George was playing in the front of the townhouse and Sara was in the upstairs bedroom—down for a nap.

What happened next nearly cost me the rest of this story:

George (*entering the open front door*): "Saywa [he had a lisp] is outside cryin'!"
Robin: "No, she's not; she's upstairs taking a nap."
George: "Uh uh—I just seen her. She fell in the bushes."
Robin and Jeff: "*WHAT!!!???*"

A rush out the door revealed Sara crawling out, clothed in only a shredded diaper, from a small and now much maligned yaupon holly. Other than a few scratches, she was fine and oblivious to the PTSD that was activating in my fragile mind. *Run, somewhere, . . . anywhere— NOW!!*

Our toddler had somehow managed to slip out of her crib to the open second-story window and push out the screen, had crawled on the ledge and had either jumped or fallen out. The potential tragedy overwhelmed me to the point that I couldn't find the language to process it. I just wanted to run.

After securing everyone back in their assigned positions for the Sunday afternoon, I made an excuse to leave. I may have mumbled something about needing to talk to my sponsor; at any rate I got away from all of this as quickly as the four-cylinder Dodge could propel me.

I had followed every recovery plan I knew of. I had trained for this type of event in treatment and had some small store of experience in the day-to-day stresses of early recovery. But this felt HUGE. I wanted a drink, *needed* a drink, . . . needed oblivion.

A phone call to my sponsor revealed that he was unavailable. I dropped by the house of a couple of recovering guys and shared with them my experience and desire to drink. They seemed to shrug it off, and after about an hour I left. Driving to a bar on the other side of town, I returned to the futile engagement of mind against drink. Historically I had never won these battles, always knowing deep inside that resistance was useless. But I raised every mental defense I could muster, even as another part of me engaged the clutch and followed a plan toward intoxication.

Alcohol couldn't be sold on Sundays except in private clubs. This was an easy workaround, and I knew the people at this bar. I pulled the truck alongside an ATM that sat adjacent and in view of my new refuge. Sweating, crying and battling with everything in me, I cried out to God even as the money was being disbursed from the machine. "*GOD, HELP ME!*"

Bill Wilson speaks about this phenomenon in his book *Alcoholics Anonymous*. This experience is so common that it may be said to amount to a rite of passage for every alcoholic earnestly seeking recovery: "Once more: the alcoholic at certain times has no effective mental defense against the first drink. Except in a few rare cases, neither he nor any other human being can provide such a defense. His defense must come from a Higher Power" (page 43).

I believe this to be a core principle of human freedom. The addict is a tangible example of our human condition, separated from God. We have no freedom of our own. Instead, we operate within a severely limited range of choices that are ultimately deterministic in nature. That is, our choices and responses are in a sense all predetermined; they are directly affected by a series of previous choices and established patterns of behaviors, so that we aren't fully free to make choices outside of the scope of these influences. Think "domino" affect.

For an addict this is especially evident. We can't truly be free from the bondage of obsession and compulsion. The determinants "drive" us to use drugs or drink, even when doing so contradicts our true desires, values and morals. For example, it's important to me to be a good and reliable father, one who protects and provides. However, I can't live up to these desires because the obsessive-compulsive nature of my addiction has severely limited my freedom. Because of this determinant influence, my freedom is held in bondage and I can't operate beyond these influences—I will drink and damage my role as a father despite my sincere intentions to do otherwise.

In order to obtain true freedom from addiction we must be in a position to choose God over our idols. We must be free to really decide what it is we want and then exercise our will toward that end. In order to freely choose we need His help, His power. Divine intervention. We need free will. This is known as libertarian freedom—the ability to make choices that are removed from all of these "determining" (or predetermining) factors. Choices that can go either way, left or right, in the direction of acceptance or denial. At some point in our spiritual journey God provides this ability; he enables us to ultimately determine our choice to accept or reject Him. This is a beautiful application of justice and mercy, grace and forgiveness.

At one point during those fateful moments, with my attention briefly and miraculously altered, I happened to look down upon a small placard Robin had given me, wedged into a crack in my dashboard—something placed there at the point of an optimistic insight along the way. The placard reads:

Don't Quit

When things go wrong, as they sometimes will,
When the road you're trudging seems all uphill,
When the fund are low
And the debts are high
And you want to smile, but you have to sigh,
When care is pressing you down a bit—
Rest if you must, but don't you quit.

Life is queer with its twists and turns,
As every one of us sometimes learns,
And many a person turns about
When they might have won had they stuck it out.
Don't give up though the pace seems slow—
You may succeed with another blow.
Often the struggler has given up
When he might have captured the victor's cup;
And he learned too late when the night came down,
How close he was to the golden crown.
Success is failure turned inside out—
So stick to the fight when you're hardest hit—
It's when things seem worst that you mustn't quit.

Like the thrust of a coastal breeze rolling into a fogbank, the powerful delusion and obsession immediately shifted and then lifted. I was acutely aware of my dilemma. The belt of insanity that had bounded my thinking lifted, and I quickly sped away from the ATM and bar, driving directly to my sponsor's house. After an emotional debriefing he both cautioned and congratulated me, and I returned home to Robin, nearly seven hours later. With no cell phones I hadn't called her in my crisis. She was welcoming and grateful to see me, albeit shaken. I had dodged the bullet that seemed aimed at my entire destiny. If I had taken that drink, all would have been lost. The tortuous life of addiction would have retuned, and I would have acquired new hostages to bring into the decimation of my life. But something was different—a miraculous intervention had changed the course of this assault; an unaccustomed power had been released. I had actually exercised the freedom to choose in the microseconds of this whirlwind. I could exercise my will in conjunction with my true desire. In that brief moment God intervened and created some sort of cosmological space in which I could maneuver. I could think and choose—choose life and sobriety, but only when I could see the goals clearly, removed from the veil of addictive thinking.

I was exhausted and grateful, feeling as though I had passed some kind of test.

This event revealed three distinct principles/lessons surrounding my recovery:

1. God is who He says He is and will do what He says He will do. He is powerful and He cares. He will protect, deliver, rescue and provide. I instinctively reached out (where had that come from?) and called for His help. No formal or pious prayer, just the plea of a desperate man. The placement of that inspirational placard on my dashboard had been no accident, and it had served for me as a life preserver in a sea of insanity.
2. I would have to fight for it, remain intentional and persevere through tough times as a matter of my commitment to live.
3. I needed to learn the language of my feelings and experiences to enable me to assert control and healing over my addictive thoughts and emotions.

The lessons and confidence extracted from this experience launched me into unprecedented growth in my recovery program. I learned to live in the rhythmic cycles of day-to-day sobriety. I would go on to complete my Certificate of Human Services and stay on to pursue an Associate's Degree in Psychology. The rhythm of work, recovery and academics seemed to fit my energy level and interest.

Robin and I saved some money and, with the help of my ever-generous mother (who cosigned the loan), purchased a used mobile home—our first "house," as it were. The extensive renovation needed didn't deter us, and we set in motion our family future within this modest transition.

As a side benefit I was given the second chance to fill a role that had been both essential to and absent from my life. You will recall from an earlier chapter that I had lost my biological children and parental rights due to drinking. Being a dad has been one of the most restorative roles in my recovery. I had been given the opportunity, through the grace of God, to raise two children with Robin. I was a good father. Looking back, I'm gratified to say that I made the most of it, through every demand and sacrifice. I've been blessed to know and be validated in this role. I'm a better man for it.

It hasn't always been easy to let go of what I lost (my biological children) and embrace the gift God gave me in this second chance. Shame and inadequacy dogged me for years. The internal dialogue of "Who do you think you are, acting like a *dad*?" would threaten to rob me of this gift. Redemption and restoration can be like that sometimes. They require us to step in and take ownership of God's grace and of our own glory. We have to declare the truth—that by God's grace we *are* new people! We deserve to receive what God chooses to call us to. We have a responsibility to ourselves and others to take this and use it for His glory and for our own restoration.

Aided by food stamps, Medicaid and part-time employment, we were able to survive and grow with the generous opportunity society and God—or should I say society *through* God?—had provided us. The road was challenging and, at times, very tiring. But gratitude, determination and optimism flowed from this rich experience.

Reflections Questions

The author describes a scene during which he nearly relapses on alcohol, but God miraculously intervenes through a small sign on his dashboard.

1. Have you ever experienced a rescue, or even an unlikely "coincidence," that could only be explained as supernatural intervention? If so, what happened?
2. Do you believe God can and does speak to you through people, places, things or experiences in your day-to-day life? Why so, or why not?
3. Can we cooperate with God's will? Or does He determine our future choices for us? Please explain your answer.

11

GAINING TRACTION

D aily life was a packed ritual of children, school, work and recovery. We had formed some very strong relationships within our twelve-step community, and all of life seemed to overlap into the intimate circles of our recovering environment and friends.

I continued in school toward an Associate's Degree and performed part-time landscaping work. Robin had acquired a job delivering *Auto Trader* magazines. Yard sales were a great source of clothing and gifts, and cookouts were frequent, with children and adults (sometimes difficult to differentiate) swarming our small yard. I played guitar (to the angst of my gracious audiences) with a couple of guys and found this to be a welcome release for my pent-up emotional energy. Life was simple and good, pure and fulfilling.

As I was nearing the completion of my degree, two significant events formed the foundation of my career and family life:

1. With persistent effort I obtained a job as a residential assistant at the local detox unit, the same one at which I had been a frequent patient.

2. Robin and I were married.

The new vocation was an amazing result from my efforts at school and sobriety. I was making minimum wage ($3.35/hour), and my first paycheck of $36, printed on government letterhead, felt like a citation award. I was thrilled and grateful, noting to my coworker, "I can't believe I am getting paid for this."

As the new guy on the unit in an entry-level position, I had to work rotating shifts on a day-to-day basis. It wasn't uncommon to work the morning shift, followed by the midnight shift the next day with the second (3:00 p.m.) shift on its heels. This can be troublesome for a person in early recovery because it negatively affects appetite, sleep patterns and recovery activity schedules. To successfully navigate this challenge it is critical to design, implement and evaluate a plan and schedule that accommodates these needs. With the use of a calendar and some timely effort, I designed a weekly plan that would accommodate the priority of my sobriety. I have always guarded this with the intensity of a man who knows his life depends on it. Because I was accommodating my own needs *first*, I was also able to see to the needs of others (employer, spouse, family and friends). It always amazes me how this paradox works!

My enthusiasm and skills set were recognized and rewarded by my superiors. Within six weeks I was promoted from residential assistant to assessment counselor. I had a knack for getting people to talk and to capture their information within a succinct narrative.

I was prone to assume that my clients were as invested in their recovery as I was—a naiveté that could lead to projecting an overly optimistic treatment plan with little potential for being followed. With time and clinical supervision, however, I was able to hone my skills to become a much more effective substance abuse counselor. Within 18 months I was again promoted to the residential treatment unit—a 12-bed coed program for adults struggling with severe addiction problems.

I could write a small book on the adventures and experiences I encountered within this timeframe. My vocational star was rising, and I seemed to be gaining a reputation as a savvy and reliable counselor. The detoxification had provided a variety of professional learning experiences that served to shape my abilities.

A typical Sunday

We called this particular day of the week Suicide Sunday. The morning shift in the detox unit also served as the main crisis line for almost every cry for help from the community. After a Friday and Saturday night of cocaine binging, a distraught voice on the other end of the phone would convey the desperation and hopelessness of their existence, exacerbated by severe dopamine depletion.

Many people think it's the drug itself that induces the euphoria that's the end goal of addiction. Actually, it's the effect of the drug upon the brain's neurochemistry that produces this result. The electro-chemical transmitters are a balance of various chemicals that produce a myriad of sensations, including those of wellbeing, peace and contentment. When a substance like cocaine is ingested, it "floods" the brain with excessive amounts of dopamine, causing euphoria and a sense of excitement that's beyond compare. But the exhilaration comes with consequences. Think of squeezing a sponge repeatedly until it's nearly dry.

The problem is that it depletes the already limited available amount of this critical element while also stopping the brain from producing more; it's tricked into believing that an excess amount is present. Given this depletion, along with the lack of dopamine reproduction, the rebound effect is an excruciating experience of deep and prolonged depression. So intense is this feeling that the craving for more of the drug is intensified to a state of frenzy. People will sacrifice literally anything (their body, money, values) just to get more of the drug to avert the intense and debilitating "crash." Once the supply of the drug is interrupted they're left despondent, in a hopeless state of clinical depression.

When someone calls on Sunday morning they're usually coming off one of these binges. Talking someone through the initial steps to safety is serious business. As is often the case, we had more calls than bed availability, so an additional challenge was getting people connected with alternative help without the benefit of dealing with them in person. A caller might mention having a gun in hand (why do cocaine addicts feel the need to arm themselves?)—fully prepared to pull the trigger against their head. Children could sometimes be heard in an adjoining room. More than once I had to navigate a conversation on one line while directing law enforcement to the residence on the other—an effort to intervene to save lives.

Working this type of shift afforded me numerous opportunities to work with the "worst of the worst"—those late-stage addicts and alcoholics who would cycle and recycle through jails, treatment centers and homeless shelters. Families had long since discarded these people in response to their own desperate need for survival and sanity. Some of the callers were running from the police. Others needed a place to get off the street, especially in the winter months. Once in a while someone sincerely committed to sobriety would appear on the line, most often known as a "chronic relapser."

Relapse is the process of regression, a "backward" movement interrupting the forward trajectory of recovery. Once someone has committed to the acceptance of their addiction and begins making significant lifestyle changes and commitment toward healing, a paradigm shift sets in that begins the process of a personality change. I mentioned this earlier in the developmental model of recovery section when I described that "AHA!" moment: "Oh my God, I *am* one [an addict or alcoholic]!" Denial breaks down, desperation sets in and willingness brings about a concerted effort to engage in the process of change.

This can take the form of several overt activities; examples include engaging in a twelve- step support group (AA, NA), enrolling in a treatment program or moving into a recovery residence. The process can also include discontinuing certain activities: no longer hanging out in bars or associating with old using/drinking friends, discarding drug paraphernalia and eliminating all alcohol use and access. Even subtle changes faithfully applied can prove effective—like changing one's route home from work to avoid temptation.

All of this serves as a platform for constructing a new life. The transformation is dramatic and extensive, as well as absolutely necessary for survival and any real chance at relief. But it's also disruptive and requires sacrifice. Consequently, abstinence and recovery often follow on the heels of these efforts. Some folks are fortunate enough to build upon this and acquire lifelong sobriety on the first genuine attempt. My wife is one of those fortunate souls.

More often, however, recovery entails a process of trial and error. What separates *relapse* from *repeated experimentation* are the levels of commitment and overt change (evidenced by genuine acceptance of the condition and implications of addiction), followed by consistent, overt lifestyle changes. *This is recovery.* Anything less is merely someone trying to control their own use or determine whether or not they really are "one of those drunks."

For one-third of the "recovering" population, chronic relapse is a significant problem. Cycles of sobriety and relapse can frustrate and deplete even the most determined efforts. Why can't these people, who seem to follow all the instructions, suggestions and directions and who make a concerted effort to apply these concepts to their lives, gain long-term sobriety?

Research has shown that there's a trend within this trend. To get an idea of how many people might be affected by chronic relapse issues, let's look at a statistic from Alcoholics Anonymous:

According to AA's General Service Office in NYC, as of January 2012 there were an estimated 1.4 million members in the US and Canada and 2.1 million worldwide. An estimate is used because AA groups report neither membership details nor numbers. The above estimate comes from a tri-annual survey of AA members. Due to anonymity and the aforementioned non-reporting by groups, there are *no confirmed* members of AA. (Wiki Answers: "How Many People in Alcoholics Anonymous?; for further information see http://www.aa.org/lang/en/en_pdfs/smf-53_en.pdf for official AA report.)

So using a worldwide estimate of 3.5 million recovering people, we can extrapolate as follows:1/3 (chronic relapse prevalence) x 3.5 million people (in AA) = 1,155,000 chronic relapsers.

And that's just those affiliated with Alcoholics Anonymous.

So what's going on with over a million people in Alcoholics Anonymous alone who are struggling to acquire lifelong sobriety? Since you're reading this, your verbal or mental response will, unfortunately, go unnoticed by me. I will, therefore, voice the answer to which I've been subtly—well, okay, maybe not all that subtly—leading you toward.

Let me start by clarifying what *isn't* going on. Please don't take this as a barometer for the effectiveness—or lack thereof—of this program. Alcoholics Anonymous works—for most people most of the time. Cynics and naysayers want to disparage AA by compiling false data and anecdotal testimonies from disillusioned participants. In lieu of the AA approach they'll propose some other solution that either costs money or doesn't require the sacrifice of ego that AA does. Some even promote moderation or control in lieu of sobriety. A quick Google search on what happened to a particular leader of this type of group can clue you in to the fatal results of that experiment.

Nor is any lack of sincerity, determination or effort on the part of AA's serious participants a factor. Chronic relapsers often work harder than those who don't struggle in this manner—perhaps more diligently than any other clients. They tend to work harder, though not necessarily smarter—a picture of much effort accompanied by little, if any, strategy. To their defense they don't know what to do differently.

It's important to recognize that chronic relapsing is a sign of neither insanity nor inability. Such relapsers begin to believe that there's something innately wrong with them—that they're incapable of receiving the beautiful gift of sobriety. As they recycle through the twelve-step programs and treatment centers, offering a resigned "Here I am again" with no gain in insight as to why this is continually occurring, they may sense the dejection of those around them, voicelessly relegating them to the "hopeless case" category. They begin to feel like the proverbial leper.

What *is* going on may be attributable to one of three issues:

1. Head trauma (traumatic brain injury): Whether before, during or after the onset of addiction, this is a common factor contributing to recovery impairment. For no other reason than that addicts either fall a lot or get hit in the head through altercations, accidents, etc., this creates a significant impairment in terms of emotional management, cognitive ability and concentration.
2. Psychological trauma: Sexual abuse, physical abuse or severe emotional or physical neglect can create fractures within the soul and form unconscious mandates/injunctions that drive self-defeating attitudes and behaviors.
3. Mental illness—and consequent impairment of emotional and possibly cognitive ability to grasp and manage abstract concepts—may come into play.

Any of these issues can be overcome with appropriate therapy, medication and the acquisition of adaptive skills. Relapse prevention training can help build effective coping strategies. The combination of professional help, personal application and a strong support system can result in prolonged periods of productive and healthy recovery from the devastating cycle of addictive behaviors. Many go on from there to attain lifelong sobriety.

I found that working with the chronically relapsing population was both challenging and exceptionally rewarding. Thanks to some excellent training and abundant field experience, I've been fortunate to be part of some inspiring and redemptive success stories by folks who had both given up and been written off by others as "hopeless."

Reflection Questions

This chapter addresses the issues associated with relapse in addictive disease. Please keep in mind that addiction can constitute more than chemical dependency. This catchall term can include behavioral addictions to, for example, gambling, food, nicotine, sex or the hoarding of physical possessions.

1. What do you think about someone who returns to addictive use or other self-destructive behaviors after they've managed to quit for a while?
2. In your opinion, is addictive behavior always indicative either of moral failure or a lack of willpower, or do you think there may be other factors involved? Please explain.

12

MARRIAGE AND FAMILY

With a full-time job and benefits I felt as though I could be a responsible partner in a serious and committed relationship. Up to this point in recovery, both my life and my reliability factor had improved tremendously. However, I still wasn't confident in my ability to provide. This was a critical and core need in terms of my masculinity—one that played a wounding role in my life for decades.

To be honest, there were some practicalities in my decision to propose marriage. We were outgrowing our need for Social Service benefits (Medicaid and food stamps), and it made sense for Robin and me to connect our futures and security through the civil and spiritual contract of marriage. We were deeply in love—and navigating life within a healthy, intimate relationship. We were convinced within our hearts that we were right for each other.

I was learning to be a father, a real dad. When I reread this section for my editor, I edited out *"father again."* I had never before understood how to be good dad. Almost any adult male can father a child, but it takes an authentic man to be a dad—one who is patient, kind, strong, protective and willing to admit imperfection, while owning the responsibility to improve. A good dad is a provider who sacrifices his time, talent and attention to the ever-demanding needs of his children. He knows when it's okay to say yes and when it's necessary to say no. He isn't afraid to discipline and is wise enough to know how. He learns flexibility and, if he doesn't have a natural sense of humor, acquires one along the way. He is at the same time tender and fierce, nurturing and firm.

I was reminded of the humor required to be an effective parent during an unexpected afternoon visit by a sheriff's deputy. A rather monotonous midmorning was disrupted by an intrusive banging on the front door, which quickly revealed an intense-looking law enforcement officer on the steps, asking—rather, demanding—to know what was going on! My wide-eyed and stunned look of ignorance only seemed to escalate the intensity of the inquisition. It sounds shallow to respond to this type of situation with a "don't what you're talking about" defense. They hear it all the time.

In this case I was a bit shaken both by the intrusion and by my claustrophobic proximity to a police officer. Years of experience in all too similar situations had convinced me that such encounters (or confrontations!) invariably resulted in a bad outcome—usually an escorted ride to the local pokey. I felt as though I had seen all of this before and internally knew it wouldn't end well.

Further explanation on his part revealed that a 911 call had been made from the house, with the caller abruptly hanging up. Naturally this solicited a mandatory health and welfare check; hence the guy at my door. It wasn't me who had made the call, and the only other two occupants in the house at the time were my son and the cat. Having had some college under my belt, along with a couple years of clear-thinking sobriety, I tried to visualize how and why the cat would have called for help. Who had trained him about 911, and how in the world was he able to use those massive, furry paws to cuddle and dial a phone? Besides, now that I'd thought it through I recalled letting him out the door earlier that morning. Once that option was dismissed, it was easy to deduce that my son (George) had made the call.

A quick summons to the front door and further interrogation by the police officer solicited the sheepish confession we were both looking for. George had been playing around with the phone and probably experimented with a recent school lesson on 911 services. Yep, it works.

After a firm lesson by the deputy and an "amen" from my pew, we closed the door and had a pretty good laugh. This story gets retold on occasion with friends and family as one of those fond memories of raising kids. Even now, while in the thick of the parenting fray, I could laugh at these things and begin to see the personalities developing in my son and daughter. Cool stuff.

Marriage wasn't only the right thing but one of the best outcomes of my sobriety. Robin was and is beautiful. I married above my natural ability. Our faith was distorted and immature, but we had enough bearing to know and love God. Out of some adherence to my Christian heritage, I sought out the services of an Episcopal clergy member. We wanted our marriage to be more than a civil union. Turns out we didn't meet the qualifications to be wed in the church and therefore were denied this opportunity. Several calls to other mainline denominations yielded the same results. We were stuck . . . or thought we were.

We had seen a small chapel alongside a route we often took to recovery meetings. On our inquiry the pastor agreed to meet with us. He was a large, gentle and attentive man who took the time to ask caring questions, while learning about our lives and stories. I will always be grateful for his patience and wisdom. He understood my aversion to (more accurately, my confusion about) Christian culture and simply asked that we consider seeking more church involvement as our marriage evolved. He didn't force anything and exhibited the attributes of love and tolerance without compromising his commitments. He agreed to marry us. We filled the small chapel with mostly recovering friends and held a potluck reception dinner at a local apartment complex pool area, compliments of my buddy, who doubled as the maintenance man there.

It was a beautiful service, filled with the love of a passionate and grateful couple and shared with close friends. It's fortunate that we have *both* our memories to reflect upon this wonderful event: the videotape of our ceremony was inadvertently used later on to record an episode of *Dragon Ball Z*, compliments of the same George who had experimented with calling 911 in the previous anecdote. This indiscretion was discovered after the parental statute of limitations had passed, as in a couple of years later. Yep, parenting will change you for the better, drive you insane, . . . or ultimately both.

Reflection Questions

The author develops an ability to pursue and sustain deep relational commitments; he experiences a renewed power for moral choice and a restoration of his masculinity and experiences psychological and spiritual healing.

1. What do you think about "second" chances in life?
2. Does this apply to those who don't "deserve" them? Please explain.

Have you been given a "do over" in any areas of your life? What were they? What has been the result?

13

PROSPERITY AND GROWTH

Vocational and educational pursuits continued for both Robin and myself. We began looking for a house to accommodate our growing family. It was during the course of this experience that I learned how good God is with the details.

It's easy to fall into the trap of assuming that our little prayers and requests are just that—*little*. I had developed an unconscious theology that God was too big, too busy and too indifferent to look after my miniscule needs and wants. Sure, I had seen Him come through with the big stuff—sobriety, rescue, bail money (was that one really Him, or my manipulation?). Our current desire for a house, though, seemed to fall within the "Oh brother, what *now??*" category in terms of God's demanding schedule (I could visualize a slight sign with a tolerant eye roll). I held Him at much too much distance to consider that He'd come through with the non-urgent desires of my heart—abundantly, joyfully and consistently.

I'm not promoting a prosperity gospel but want to simply state here that God *does* care and that He knows me so well He sends gifts that could only have been custom-designed for me.

Personalized, specialized and specific, leaving no doubt that He both knows and cares about my needs *and* my desires.

It all started with the concept of efficiency. Our little mobile home was a hotbox in the sizzling summers of Charleston, South Carolina. I pondered the idea of adding some storm windows to better insulate the home. After estimating the price, though, I somehow leaped to the conclusion that trading up to a "real" house was a good idea.

We began an extensive search (internet wasn't yet a reality) that involved a lot of driving around. A friend in recovery (also a realtor) helped guide us to the homes we could afford. We both had jobs and steady paychecks, but aside from a car (cosigned for us by my mother) and the payoff on a tool shed we had established no credit history. My fiscal record was filled with late and nonpayment "hits," adding to our questionable status as a sensible credit risk. It takes real money and, usually, credit to acquire a home. Our odds were slim, but this didn't deter our optimism and enthusiasm.

We landed upon a home that had all of the looks of suburban America—split level, nice yard, cul de sac and young families all around. It was a "VA Repo," meaning that it had fallen into foreclosure. The Veteran's Administration held the lien at the time, so the purchase process involved bidding. It was possible to get in with arrangements as simple as a $500 down payment. We put in an offer and held our collective breath in hopeful anticipation. We both had a strong sense that this would be our next home!

When the bidding results were announced several weeks later, though, we were dismayed to discover that we had come in fourth in the bidding. Second place can mean a remote possibility of getting the home in the event the primary bidder drops out. Because of the exhaustive screening involved in submitting bids, however, these homes almost always end up in the hands of the highest bidder. A fourth-place ranking stated simply "We saw your bid and you ain't even close."

This outcome was puzzling to both of us; we had followed all the steps we knew to do in our spiritual life. As part of recovery we were following a daily devotional, as well as the application for each day's reflection, intended to help us seek God in our daily walk, lives and needs. Finding a home would meet a legitimate need, and we both firmly believed God was leading us to this provision. We had felt so confident that this little house was going to be ours that we had mentally already moved in. This kind of disappointment can constitute a painful lesson on the dangers inherent in writing the script before God is finished doing His part. We had unwittingly been caught in another form of self-sufficiency, working apart from—and evidently ahead of—God. Still we persisted in the belief that this was *our* home and felt a heavy loss at the news.

Several weeks passed. We responded by following a distant lead on a new construction home. It had the potential to meet our needs in a nice, developing subdivision and was affordable, though lacking some of the amenities we were seeking in a true home. In our minds and hearts this was simply a house. We were settling for something else in lieu of our dream.

We signed a contract to proceed. But the very next morning I received a call from my former realtor. After a brief chat he asked me somewhat casually, "Do you still want that house?" I was stunned, silent. What did he mean? He went on to say that all three prior bidders had either failed to meet the qualifications or had dropped out of the running—an unprecedented event in his 30 years of real estate experience. The number four bidder was now the number one contender—so did we want it?!

"Yes, . . . but wait; we can't—just signed a contract last night on another house!" *We're too far down the trail—no way to turn this thing around. Ouch—we were going to miss our dream home because we had jumped too soon, had taken matters into our own hands out of disappointment, doubt and self-determination!*

Instead, as you savvy readers may have foreseen, a quick call resulted in a gracious release from the new construction contract. Instantly we were on the path to our dream home. We closed in 45 days and celebrated on July 4, 1994, with pizza in a vacant living room. We were *home!* God is good, in this case deftly working out those details in a twist we weren't soon to forget!

This move provided two developmental milestones in our lives. Socioeconomically, we were moving into a cultural setting we had formally considered off limits for us—belonging with those "normal" people. People with jobs, families, mortgages—people who were, according to some nebulous but easily detectable formula, "doing life." The neighborhood was middle class; our ascension from poverty and social assistance had significantly progressed in just three years. Now we were learning to manage financial and vocational success. Spiritually, we were learning that God is in everything, but on a scale beyond what either of us had formerly begun to understand.

Twelve-step recovery is a major steppingstone into learning and applying a spiritual dimension to life. Addiction is such a complex and destructive force that it requires a drastic and comprehensive process to acquire deliverance and restoration—a process embodying mind, body and spirit. God gets us there through prevenient grace and provides us with the freedom to choose. We can reject the opportunity for recovery and continue in self-defeating cycles of addiction or, even worse, mental and emotional anguish. Or we can choose His will and grow in all those areas toward which He beckons—experiencing more freedom, a fuller life, greater purpose and contentment. The 12 steps are a methodical process that revamp the distorted mental and emotional constructs and open the spiritual pathways to full restoration. They constitute a spiritual program with a practical application.

Still, the first steps are very rudimentary; as drastic as these concepts are, they're at the same time no-frills basic and fundamental. Bill Wilson, the cofounder of Alcoholics Anonymous, refers to the association as a "spiritual kindergarten." To remain within the broad spiritual "door" of seeing God only as a "Higher Power" is comparable to limiting one's access to the fullness, conveniences and provisions of a larger home. I don't live on my front porch; it only serves as an entryway to the better parts of my home. There's the den, where I relax. The bedroom, where I rest. The kitchen, where my sustenance is derived in the form of great meals. The bathroom, where I meet my hygiene and biological needs. The living room, where gatherings of family and friends feed my soul. The attic, where I store my treasures and memories, and the office/study, where I organize and administer the responsibilities of my home and even cultivate my mind and spirit in communion with and in an enhanced knowledge of God. I would never dream of trying to accomplish all of this from my front porch.

Yet I've seen so many recovering people trying to live out the complexities of life from just that vantage point—limiting themselves to the basics of the twelve-step programs. Sure, you can do it. But *why?!* Its confines are cramped, limited, constraining—painfully inadequate. Yet how often don't we settle for the comfort of what is familiar in order to avoid the discomfort of the risky and uncertain? Listening to and following God can appear to be just that—a calculated but less than guaranteed proposition for us. Yet He asks each of us, specifically and individually, to take the risk and move toward the uncertainty of His call. To quote C. S. Lewis, "He is dangerous, but He is good."

So many folks choose not to venture beyond the safety and familiarity of twelve-step groups in the direction of the calling God has placed upon their hearts. The result is a stagnant life. This is easy to see. Such people may cycle through periodic relapses. They may remain "clean and sober" but hold on to deep emotional and psychological wounds that drive cyclical, self-defeating beliefs and behaviors. Their relationships are often conflicted, and they suffer from a pervasive sense of isolation inadequacy and loneliness. They're often compulsive in other behaviors—"lesser" addiction-related behaviors that tend to become more and more problematic over time, like overeating, overspending, sexual compulsions or gambling, all often leading to depression. Clouds of self-centeredness or codependency pervade their lives. Some of this is met with despair, but the more likely reactions are opposition (not to the negative behaviors but to people and expectations that may get in their way), anger and defiance. Their motto is "At least I ain't . . . " (you fill in the blank with drinking, stealing, lying, . . . or whatever). This is a current comparison to a former life, a rationalization for poor choices skirting the real issues by focusing on how much worse the situation could be. The tipoff rationalizations, often delivered in a glib manner, may be "Hey, I ain't perfect!" or (this one's my favorite) "If you don't like it, that's your problem." Try to argue with that!

I invariably try to challenge this when I can. Maybe you are someone in recovery who has slowed or stagnated in their spiritual growth and holds this position. At whatever stage you find yourself, consider seriously my question *"How is all this working for you?"* Better yet, how about if I ask those privileged to live with you (or, to drop to a lower common denominator, *try to live* in your presence)—your kids, spouse, employer or coworkers. Most of these folks have been bullied into a passive, and often a smoldering, silence. Others have given in to a despondent resignation that what they see in you is as good as it gets. Maybe they resort to hoping against hope for a distant miracle or enduring the disappointment through indulging their own addiction or some other payoff. Victims become volunteers, . . . and there's *always* a payoff. I believe we owe it to ourselves and others to be diligent in our growth. Attitudes of self-righteousness and defiance only serve to create a toxic perspective that spoils the freedom and fruit of recovery. Sure, we might get by with it, but at what cost to ourselves and others?

Through this home acquisition the two of us were learning that God both leads and provides. He's attentive to the specifics and delights in doling out those extra amenities and frills. Not based on our accomplishments but on His endless delight in us.

> The LORD your God is with you,
> the Mighty Warrior who saves.
> He will take great delight in you;
> in his love he will no longer rebuke you,
> but will rejoice over you with singing.
>
> (Zephaniah 3:17, NIV)

We were also learning to be responsible, to be good stewards of His gifts. There was a new, cooperative and empowering dynamic in terms of our relationship with God. We trusted Him and He trusted us to do well, to handle it.

We had numerous experiences and could tell endless stories from the five-year tenure in our dream home. This season was for us a slice of quintessential American life and optimism—quaint house, good friends and neighbors, working middle class, safety and freedom, opportunity and hope. This would prove to be our longest tenure in one living space for another 15 years. More than a place, this home still holds for us fond and enduring memories. I would rate this as one of the best seasons of our lives.

Reflection Questions

1. Do you think God actually pays attention to the seemingly minute details of our lives? How not, or how so?
2. Do you think that what is important to us is important to God, or is he too busy / disconnected / above and beyond us to notice?
3. What has been your experience with God in the details of your life? Can you point to one or two serendipities in your experience that just had to be more than coincidence?
4. What does the author mean by not subscribing to a "prosperity gospel"? What are your thoughts on this issue?

14

THE TRIAL

On a seemingly random weekday at work I received a legal summons by a judicial court server, who seemed a little too eager to deliver an additional bonus of attitude and intimidation with the paperwork. You never know what you're going to see when you open one of these things. They simply approach you and ask "Are you so-and so . . . ?" Your quizzical response conveys a mixture of flattery (Why, yes, I am!) and fear (Who wants to know?). Am I winning a lottery or am I a target for the hit man? (My wife is taking our disagreements much too seriously.)

As I open the summons I see that I have been awarded an opportunity to serve on a jury trial in General Sessions court. This is big time—the Super Bowl equivalent of the South Carolina criminal justice system. Career criminals work diligently to reach this summit. After years of screwing around with petty crimes, they launch their destiny with the real possibility of long-term incarceration with a felony charge that brings out the best and worst of the criminal justice system. Some enjoy the public recognition so much, in fact, that they reoffend just for the chance to do it all again. It's quite an event. We tie up serious time and money to somehow take a simple concept of truth and mangle it through an oratorical and judicial manufacturing process that would make Henry Ford marvel at the final product.

Good news for me—I'm to get paid from my job while I'm there. Being an inveterate multi-tasker, I figure this will give me a chance to catch up on some reading for the approaching start of graduate school.

For those of you who don't know how this process goes, allow me to illustrate:

A judicial calendar holds the docket, or agenda, for the trials that will be scheduled for a session. These sessions may run several weeks at a time. Those on the docket who will plead guilty get processed through quickly—a judge hears their plea, a lawyer or the defendant explains why it was all a big mistake, and the judge renders a verdict. Pretty straightforward. Not necessarily an element of truth in any of this, but an expedient method nonetheless for moving things along.

Then there's the jury trial. Television has enlightened its viewing audience with shows featuring the likes of Judge Mathis or Judge Judy—part of the evolution of the esteemed forerunner *The People's Court*. Real intellectual treasure in this stuff. But (hope I'm not bursting any bubbles here) most of this is acting. Not to be confused with the posturing that happens continually in "real court" but actual (paid) acting. The participants are paid to illustrate actual cases that have been filed. It's all entertainment; no one goes to jail, and convincing participants might just land a spot on an episode of *Days of Our Lives*.

The real jury trial in General Sessions court includes all the players. That's because real prison (as opposed to jail) time hangs

The Trial

in the balance. Lawyers make or break their careers in this venue. The local assistant prosecutor is gunning for the top solicitor job, or, better yet, for a shot at that school board post. The defense attorneys (usually former assistant prosecutors who didn't make the school board cut) are vying for notoriety. Having spent recent settlement money—wrangled from some poor shmoe's auto insurance carrier (his and our rates continue to skyrocket because of shenanigans like this)—on extensive advertising, this guy or gal has to come through with the goods to show future clients (many of whom are in the courtroom today) how outstanding he/she really is at this stuff.

The local citizens who have managed to keep their lives fairly clean and unobtrusive to the rest of society now become candidates for participation in the judicial process. Keep in mind that the only people in this process *not* getting paid are the defendant and the juror—everybody else is on the clock.

So a summons to appear in court results in several hundred people arriving to be screened in an effort to determine their viability as potential jurors for the approaching trials. The individual in this position doesn't know which trials are approaching or how long they'll likely last. For each case the defense attorney and prosecutor ask strategic questions to determine the best allies for their respective sides. Each attorney is allowed a certain number of "vetoes" to the others selections. And so it goes until the required number of jurors is picked and two alternates (backups) assigned. Some get to opt out if they can convince the judge of a good reason for them not to serve, but for the most part you can plan on sticking around. I had considered using a suggested tactic I had heard from a comedian: once under questioning he would blurt out "I can tell a guy is guilty just by looking at him!"

As we were called individually, one by one, to respond (under oath) to the questions, it became clear that I was one of those guys who could perceive things with clarity. By this I mean that the mention of my counseling background was an effective source of further inquiry, and I could tell the defense attorney wasn't at all interested in having me learn more about his client. He vetoed me almost immediately.

While I was glad not to have to hang around (wrong assumption, by the way), I at the same time felt a bit rejected. I was told to wait for another round of inquiry for another trial. So on day two I returned and was surprised to find that this initial selection process was continuing. I have no idea why, but I was recalled as a potential juror for the same trial. This time I passed muster.

By midafternoon we'd been sworn in and given juror instructions, and the trial swept into motion. It was a sexual abuse trial. The alleged perpetrator, a young male in his mid twenties, was charged with molesting two young boys (brothers), ages six and eight. He was a family friend and caretaker while the parents were at work.

Over time this supposed paragon of virtue had acquired the trust of everyone involved, and he used his proximity and the boys' vulnerability to expose them to alcohol and pornography. This morphed into an abusive pattern of indulgences perpetrated on the children, who finally reported it to the parents. An investigation and arrest followed, which had ultimately brought us all together some 12 months later.

The proceedings launched into a methodical presentation of the prosecution's case. Evidence included the "unassailable" witness of videotapes focusing in on condoms in the trashcan and empty alcohol containers. Painful testimony from the young boys revealed a consistent and traumatic pattern of seduction and abuse. Tearful but determined, they were able to narrate the sequence of events that had systematically eroded their innocence and forever altered the trajectory of their lives.

The defense attorney cross-examined but was unable to dissuade the children from their positions. This process continued with the detectives who had discovered and presented the evidence. However, when the time arrived for the defense to present its case, the drama escalated.

The 18th-century theologian John Wesley believed that the restoration of fallen man will include a renewed capacity to comprehend truth. Without (or before) restoration, this capacity is severely diminished in us, as is evidenced in all of the confusion around and in which we currently live. Truth is, things are rarely as they seem. Understanding is the ability to see things as they really are, to hold a firm grasp upon reality; to look past distortion, manipulation and incomplete information to arrive at a certainty based on clarity and fact. In the legal world of viability, a circumstance or event only has to be *possible*, not necessarily true. The concept of reasonable doubt serves as an axis point for most of the defensive arguments in any given case. So, in the end, a court session isn't about finding the truth so much as about presenting a convincing version of the event that best meets the needs of the stakeholder. It's all about raising doubt through the conveyance of an intriguing possibility. For a guilty person this is almost invariably far from the truth.

We as a jury spent the better part of a week listening to testimony and mentally sorting the evidence. One of our instructions included not talking about the case amongst ourselves until the arguments concluded and we had been sent to deliberate the evidence. This occurred on a Thursday afternoon. The 12 of us convened and began unpacking all that we had observed and experienced.

A large, rectangular table configuration allowed us to see each other clearly. The physical evidence was strategically displayed in the center if the table, occasionally catching the contemplative glance of a juror. As we settled in I was certain a unanimous verdict of guilty would emerge. The lead juror reviewed the instructions, and a poll was taken of each juror's perspective.

I can't describe my initial shock upon hearing that nine of the twelve jurors were at this early point holding to a verdict of not guilty. My first thought was "What did I miss?" I had no doubt this dude was not only guilty but "*guilty, dammit!*" Still, I managed to maintain my composure and listened patiently to each person's viewpoint. When my turn came I simply pointed out the consistencies in testimony, alleged motive and evidence. I wasn't determined to change anyone's mind but was only conveying my perspective. This went on for the rest of the day and well into Friday.

After lunch on Friday we took another poll. By now a few more people had conceded that the defendant was most likely guilty—that he had indeed perpetrated his willful desires upon those young boys. The standoff was now six (guilty) to six (not guilty). If we failed to reach a unanimous verdict we would have to agree to disagree—resulting in the ignominy of a hung jury and a mistrial, with the defendant going free. The prosecution always has the option of a retrial, but this is extremely taxing on both the victims and the system.

I felt compelled to address the ambiguity that was so pervasive in the room. An energy and clarity rose up in my spirit, and I felt confident as I took the floor to speak. Reviewing all the facts that were indisputable, we were hanging up on the disconcerting concept of reasonable doubt. Too many seemed to think that if there was any remote possibility of innocence they were compelled to vote not guilty. And there was the turning point.

With a deepened sense of authority and certainty I held up the physical evidence—bagged, thank goodness—and within the context of the boys' testimony stated that "either this guy is guilty or he's the unluckiest son-of-a-bitch I've ever met!" Silence and wide-eyed stares. Had I overstepped my bounds here?

More talking, accompanied now by head shaking. Something had broken loose. An energy arose, and the conversations sharpened.

Over the course of the next two hours a unanimous verdict of GUILTY was returned.

Jurors are not allowed access to certain information known to the rest of the court, on the context that it might bias them against making "an impartial" decision. When the prosecutor came over to talk to us afterward, she thanked us tearfully. Truth was, we were already involved in a retrial; the former had failed on some minor technicalities. Everyone in court knew the guy was guilty; only the jury had been denied that reality. If we had played it safe with a "not guilty" verdict, the perpetrator would likely have walked forever. And those impressionable young boys would have been betrayed a second time by the very authority that was supposed to protect them.

I was deeply moved by the week's events. This experience quickened the subconscious and unhealed areas of my soul surrounding my own experiences. Not so much in the detail, but in the general sense of feeling betrayed, abandoned and shamed. The wrenching and graphic testimony of those innocent boys had altered my reality—awakening within me a deep compassion and incredible heartache. My emotions would ebb and flow without notice. I cried off and on for days. Sara McLaughlin's hit song "The Arms of an Angel" repeatedly played in my mind. I had encountered a rising awareness of the universality of the pain and trauma humanity exerts against and upon its own. My own proscribed world of recovery and addiction seemed small. There was so much more going on out there, and I felt compelled to engage it.

Reflection Questions

This chapter provides a dramatic recollection of a jury trial involving two young boys, the main character's service on this jury, and the resulting impact on his soul; it also includes a tongue-in-cheek overview of court procedure; philosophical discussion on the aspects of truth; and the author's growing personal awareness of emotional pain as a universal human experience.

1. How do stories of children being hurt affect you?
2. How do you think God feels about the injustices humanity inflicts on itself?
3. Can you empathize with (feel the pain of) other people's struggles or tragedies, even when you may not personally have had experience with that particular issue?
4. Is truth for you a matter of what your personal experience happens to have been? Or are there universal, unchanging principles at play? Please explain.

15

GRADUATE SCHOOL

Throughout the previous five years I had continually pursued my education and had finished an undergraduate (bachelor's) degree in psychology. Each new educational commitment was followed by "and then I'll be finished." With the recent completion of this academic work I felt as though I had reached the pinnacle of my educational achievements and was settling into my career. Robin too had just finished her educational stint and now held a nursing license. It was time to settle into a more balanced routine.

During a random conversation with some colleagues, one of them inquired about my career goals. I was excited to inform him of my interest in management with the hope that one day I would serve as an executive director for a substance abuse facility. I was both discouraged and intrigued by his response: "You'll need a master's degree to do that."

With a recent promotion to an entry-level management position, I was learning and succeeding quickly in the world of supervision. I had a natural ability to motivate and inspire. With an understanding of the mission and the support of an empowering supervisor, I was enjoying the authority and recognition that had come with visibility.

One day another colleague laid on my desk a newspaper advertisement, along with a personal note of encouragement. The ad was promoting a graduate degree in Health Care Administration from the University of South Carolina. The accompanying note proclaimed simply "for the next Executive Director!"

I was interested and daunted at the same time. Where would the money and time come from? Would they accept me? More concerning was that up to this point I had been involved only with night school. This was a *real* university—no way, I quickly dissuaded myself, could I make it there. They'd know I was a fake.

These are the pesky voices and attitudes playing and replaying in the minds of recovered addicts and alcoholics that hold at bay many potential opportunities, disallowing them from moving beyond just that—opportunities (or, more pessimistically, pipe dreams). Without action these siren calls never materialize into anything beyond a dream—a distant hope or off-the-wall daydream. If one lingers upon these challenges without pressing through to actualization, they successfully keep her in limbo, her desires held captive by those dismissive, and seemingly insurmountable, qualifiers like "Where? When? And How?" Together these preemptive dismissals function as a coffin to contain every desire that is meant to be reality.

Fortunately I had enough experience (faith?) to inquire further. God had countless times been faithful in calling and leading me out beyond—way beyond—my acknowledged capabilities. The pattern was always the same: a desire and an intrigue followed by the dawning awareness of a real possibility. The next step, one of pure faith, would be a "push off" into uncertainty, undergirded by some level of hope and wisdom. This stepping out into risk was invariably exhilarating. Then would come the lull in certainty and the entrance of confusion, thankfully followed by staying the course, with God arriving just in time to shore me up with provision and assurance. Embedding these experiences into a practical and determined working out of one's faith is critical to navigating life with peace and assurance. This can propel one beyond their wildest imagination as to what they can indeed accomplish . . . so long as they have the assurance—you'll know it when you encounter it—that God is in it!

With a little research and a lot of effort directed toward the application process, I was accepted into the program. I found myself enrolled in graduate school—a real, bona fide graduate school—a state university, no less. Here I was, working only a few feet from the very room that had once housed my detoxing, addicted body. I was a highly respected manager within a behavioral healthcare facility . . . and now, in conjunction with that wonder, a graduate school student at a respected university. Just recollecting and recording this, even today, is humbling, as I consider what God has done in, with and for me.

Truth be told, the college orientation weekend held many negative emotions for me—those old demons of fear, doubt and shame. After the enthusiasm of applying and planning, the implementation of a goal invariably hurtles the spirit into an emotional nosedive. With possibility becoming reality, those perceived obstacles, accompanied by the resultant fear and intimidation, can no longer be held at bay. The first 15 minutes in my first class were, and remain in memory, a blur—my head was swimming in covert comparisons and self-condemnation. I looked at some of these folks—factoring in their backgrounds in medicine, insurance and banking. Highly successful people in their own right, in high-profile careers. And then there was me—a substance abuse counselor and low-level manager. What the hell was I doing here? The previous day's venture to the bookstore had initiated this downward emotional spiral. My eager spouse was enthusiastically shopping with me, sharply contrasting the growing shadows within my soul. I was heavy with shame and even embarrassment. Where had all this undeserved change come from?

I was unaware of the spiritual battles that invariably assail a child of God. I had the solid support of twelve-step recovery and a deepening path of intuitive and relational intimacy with God. But I also had deep, untouched wounds in my heart that Satan was now vigorously using to accompany his haunting tunes of hatred, inadequacy and despair. These demonic efforts manifested between my ears in the form of intimidation and a wild urge for flight. The resulting turmoil was nearly paralyzing; I couldn't shake the deep-seated feeling of gross inadequacy. Still, I had perseverance on my side, along with enough innate pride and learned fortitude to push through. I had already set this in motion, in a very public manner. No way was I backing down; I didn't want to be considered a quitter.

The players in the two-year program included myself and 17 cohorts—students who would, with me, go through the process as a team. This forced intimacy exposed me to a variety of other professionals and systems outside the recovery world, providing me with a broader and deeper perspective on life around me. This allowed me to expand my identity beyond the social and professional world of addiction.

The first year of training was intense but affirming. The curriculum provided me with a language and perspective that helped validate and sharpen my beliefs. I gained confidence that I could indeed perform graduate-level work. Year two, unfortunately, was another story. We entered into the world of finance and accounting. Many of my peers had experienced undergraduate training in this area, but my own exposure to math had included only Statistics and Algebra 1. I was in deep water!

With all the effort I could muster, I finished business finance with a less than impressive final score of 69. This was a long and painful semester, and for the first time in my seven years of recovery I had to concede failure in something. This constituted, unfortunately, more than just a course failure, threatening as it did to crash the entire graduate project. Cohorts had to move together, meaning that anyone who fell behind was eliminated from the program. In fact, we had to this point lost over half of the original hopefuls—there were just eight of us left. I was at a loss to explain why I couldn't comprehend this material. I had studied diligently, practiced and even sought tutoring. And now, in December 1998, with just eight months of classes left in quest of a degree, I was teetering on the brink of defeat.

My spiritual world was imploding in on me as well. I needed to make sense of this unforeseen development, to mesh the discordant realities of God's clear call with my current failure. I found myself overwhelmed and tearful—desperate for understanding. An impromptu meeting with a pastor helped me gain some peace and perspective. Later that very day I walked into the vacant wooded lot behind my workplace, crying out to God for answers, for direction. What to do? What was this all about—to come so far and fail now?! A few days later I was contacted by the dean of the Healthcare Administration program. I needed to come in and discuss this issue to determine whether I could remain in the program.

Turns out two other people had also failed. The department didn't like losing students and quickly came up with a plan for us to work through this hurdle. The three of us would retake the finance course concurrently with staying on track with the cohort. This meant that we would carry an additional course load while we worked through the former academic work. All three of us were already attending classes full time in conjunction with working full time. My response was ambivalent; I was partly relieved and partly discouraged, with no clear idea from what inner resources I would summon the time or energy for this extra burden. At one point prior to even beginning I was ready to quit. I was angry at the university, angry at God and angry with myself. I felt some of the old rebellion rising—a heightened sense of defiance . . . coupled with a deep sense of abandonment.

Then one morning God showed up, unannounced and without fanfare, and poured determination back into my soul. By January, the beginning of the dreaded semester, I was recommitted to the process.

These ups and downs and highs and lows have not only been fairly predictable in all of my successes but, ironically, extremely helpful. I can't claim that this is always the way God chooses to do things, but I am seeing a pattern that fits my life. Intrigue, desire, opportunity and action are typically met by fear, frustration and discouragement. This faceoff serves to draw me into something that ultimately improves my life by exposing my wounds and unresolved issues. In order to get through this turmoil, I'm forced to contend with these painful emotions, and ultimately others. Quitting may be an option, but I have somehow avoided this exit strategy. Instead I've consistently experienced God holding on to me. I've somehow learned in the process to quit fighting and rest within His grip of grace. He has indeed been gracious, allowing me to squirm and complain but never letting me squeeze out of his grasp. His determination to lead the way and bring me again and again into fullness is a beautiful illustration of His love and servant humility. At the point I let go I'm invited to participate with Him. The spiritual training wheels are removed for yet another season, and I live in the dignity of freedom, restoration and enhanced maturity.

The remaining eight months of the graduate course proved to be intensely challenging and exhausting. But I'm gratified to report that I finished . . . and finished well. I walked the graduating line with several hundred other students, in full view of my proud mother and aunt, friends, spouse and children. Another miraculous accomplishment in my growing list of recovery-oriented achievements.

During the last month of my graduate work my employer had made a decision that if I didn't accept a promotion to an essential leadership role in the agency I needed to resign or be terminated. Really—it was either take the promotion or get out.

I had seen evidence in the past of how this ultimatum had been used as a scapegoat for all the failures in leadership within the agency as a whole. I had no desire to walk into this chaos.

Looked like I was going to need a new job . . .

I had spent the previous eight years discovering and applying pragmatic spiritual concepts to my life. Learning to be honest with myself led to an effective method of identifying and correcting personality flaws that continually manifested themselves in some kind of sin. I built a strong social network, at first exclusively within the recovery community. This gradually expanded beyond the safety and familiarity of twelve-step recovery and into the expanses of the "real" world.

A daily reliance upon a conscious contact with God built intrinsic characteristics of trust, faith and obedience. I gained an instinctual ability to know and follow God's will. His direction in my life was sometimes simple and sometimes drastic. I learned that just knowing God's will wasn't enough—that I would have to sometimes relinquish my own selfish objectives. This revealed a greater self-awareness of my "hidden" nature, enabling me to bring these defects to God in order to attain a willingness to be released or healed from them. I had cringed at organized religion and for a long time had felt as though I had finally found my church home in a twelve-step fellowship. But God wasn't willing to stop there. The graduate school years overlapped with my return to an interdenominational Christian fellowship.

Reflection Questions

The author describes meeting the challenges of growth and opportunity. He gives personal examples and a launches a philosophical discussion about confronting the negative, self-defeating beliefs that plague us. He describes wrestling with failure and, with God's help, building resiliency.

1. Most people want little or no risk when they're faced with choices. What has held you back from pursuing your dreams? Or what uncertainties and risks have you had to overcome in order to pursue your dreams?
2. What internal dialogue plays out in your mind when you face doubt and uncertainty?

Application Exercise

For the next three days pay attention to your thoughts when you encounter doubt, fear or lack of confidence. Listen closely—What is being said? Where do you think this is coming from? Make note of what you hear and share this with a trusted mentor or friend. Learn ways to challenge the disconcerting assault of the interior monologue that threatens to dismantle your confidence and cooperation.

PART 2

16

LONGING FOR MORE

"You won't relent until You have it all, My heart is Yours . . . "
—From the album *Relentless* by Misty Edwards, 2007

Recovery entails so much more than stopping alcohol and/or drug use. It's more than tidying up life mistakes and upgrading moral values. It demands more than settling for good when the best is continuously within reach.

I have been immersed within the recovering community, as a recovering person myself, for more than two decades. What I see in the perceived success of some of those fortunate enough to acquire "long-term" (beyond 10 years) sobriety concerns me. There's a complacency built into the process that keeps one from growing into a fully mature human being. Too often this is eventually reflected in a regression of moral values and poor decision making. These folks seem to settle in to some ironic paradigm of self-righteousness and refuse to grow any further. What is evident in this is a growing spiritual dryness; a cynicism that this is as good as it gets; a theme of self-centeredness and self-sufficiency that is usually reinforced as they pursue materialism, recognition or power. Sometimes it's the gratification of instinctual appetites that are rationalized as acceptable behaviors: "At least I ain't drinking . . . "

An inside glimpse into the individual's family life will quickly reveal the systemic illness that continues to thrive: adult children continuing in a lifestyle of dysfunction and rebellion; spouses emotionally beaten down or enmeshed in some obscure course of pathological living (hiding or grasping at anything that appears to offer life); marital discord and alienation from intimacy. Those stuck in this mindset/lifestyle are trapped in some undefined time warp in which everyone is living out of an adolescent paradigm—impulsivity, unreliability, self-absorption and emotional/intellectual shallowness. The dysfunction is sad to watch. And it's totally unnecessary.

Bill Wilson, the cofounder of Alcoholics Anonymous, insisted that alcoholics not stop in their spiritual and relational growth. Knowing that the mind and personality of the alcoholic have been severely distorted and maligned, he made it clear that continual, progressive spiritual growth is needed in order to restore and maintain any consistent level of healing. This is an ongoing, dynamic process, requiring an inexhaustible fount of willingness and courage, desperation (yes, this can be a positive force) . . . and God.

Consider the rescue of a drowning victim, one who is enveloped by frigid waters. She may be unconscious, so emergency interventions are needed. CPR is administered, and now the pulse and breathing are back.

If her body temperature isn't quickly restored, however, she'll die of hyperthermia. To effectively bring this back up, an outside-in approach is used. There's a core heat source within the body to work with, but external measures must be brought forward to reach the critical, stabilizing temperature of 98.6 degrees.

Failure to address her needs fully and effectively may result in her staying alive but remaining comatose. What kind of life would that be, when full restoration would have been possible through additional intervention to address the hyperthermia?

This metaphor illustrates the need to do more than the minimum. It really applies to everyone, not just to addicts. If we settle for the merely good we'll live a confined life. Comatose, half alive—manifesting breath and heart rate but no fulfillment, purpose or joy.

"Where can I go from your Spirit? Where can I flee from your presence?" implored David rhetorically in Psalm 139:7.

God wants all of us. Salvation is only part of the plan. There's so much more beyond forgiveness, though if that were all we received it would be more than gracious.

The Lord may opt to rescue us from our circumstances in order to get our attention. He may use (not necessarily cause) circumstances to shake us from our apathy, cynicism or delusional self-sufficiency. He is after the fullness of our design—the sum total of all we were created to be. It matters, . . . because *we* matter.

In January 1997 I responded reluctantly but obediently to my wife's invitation to attend a marriage series at a local interdenominational church. With my learned ability to suspend judgment and the felt obligation to be a good husband, I attended the first of an eight-session series.

Church—*really?* After the long suspension of this aspect of my life, what was I doing here? The truth was that I had been searching—desperately. Searching for relief, for truth, for that elusive "more." I had been slowly but surely easing toward the deep chasms that frame the process of relapse. But how could this be? I was active in my recovery service structure. I sponsored people, served in leadership roles, attended meetings frequently, practiced thoroughly all 12 steps and surrounded myself with recovering people. All the right things one does to build and maintain a resilient and fulfilling life without the use of alcohol and drugs. All of which manifested a profound personality change and served as a template for uninterrupted, long-term recovery.

Yet a deep (so deep as to seem almost inaccessible) sense of something missing continually haunted me. Some of this was evident in the stuck points of my life, manifested by a recurring sense of fear and inadequacy and repeated "dabbling" in pornography, anger and condemnation, along with a thread of narcissistic thinking. All of this continually eroded my serenity and contentment. I sensed an uncomfortable shift in my motivation—a craving, a need for something else. Not just an adjunct to my "program" but something much more pervasive.

Sunday morning arrived, and together we made our way past the daycare section. Dropping off the kids at church had an accustomed "normal" feel—as though we were once again doing the right thing. I hadn't participated before in a contemporary church setting and was pleasantly surprised at the surroundings. No stained glass, pews, incense or choir. No ornate garments for clergy or laity. Chairs, formed in rows, faced a stage. The sermon wasn't so much a sermon as it was a presentation. I felt as though I were involved in a seminar and noticed with some surprise my ability to follow the pastor's teaching without any distraction. I also sensed the familiar "rightness" that came with walking in God's will. This seemed to be the right place to be, so we kept attending.

Thus began Robin's and my immersion and acclimation into contemporary Christian culture. This was for both of us an unforeseen pathway, the panacea for a spiritual "dryness" that had seeped into my recovery over the previous 18 months. This discomfort had brought me into a state of willingness to try something new, something different, something positive and good.

This exposure and subsequent growth, which would occur over a 15-year period, slowly began unraveling my misconceptions about Christianity and opening my heart and mind to truth, healing and restoration. I learned:

a. that the Bible is the factual representation of who God is, who we are, where we are and the good in which He is involved in our lives.
b. the spiritual disciplines of worship, tithing, prayer, study and devotion.
c. that the world, the flesh and the enemy will continuously oppose my trust in and relationship in God.

We continued to attend this church and began to meet new people along the way. I believe this helped shape our identity beyond the confines of our recovery group in a very positive way. Without apologizing for or compromising our past, we found a different common ground based on which to belong. It is healthy for individuals and couples in our position to learn to see the world in a broader and more realistic perspective. We also found that our backgrounds paralleled the universal experiences of pain, suffering and redemption. We not only belonged; we had something to offer.

Reflection Questions

This chapter provides observations on spiritual complacency in the recovering community.

1. Do you think it's enough when someone quits using alcohol/drugs or stops a self-destructive behavior? Why or why not?
2. Have you encountered spiritual complacency in your life journey? How so or how not?
3. Can a church be a place where spiritual growth can take place? What has been your experience?

17

I NEED A JOB

As mentioned earlier, I found myself unemployed and overeducated. I had to this point known only a status of "underemployed" and "undereducated," so this was a new experience. Numerous responses to job postings required a broader geographical search. I received an offer for an interview during my last week of grad school.

A company that would be opening a substance abuse treatment facility in Augusta, Georgia, was looking for an administrator. Interviews had been taking place, and I was the last one on the candidate call list. A trip to Nashville, Tennessee, led to an interview and a job offer! Before I left town to return home, I was given a startup manual for the new project. The 10-hour drive brought more concern than joy over my employment—it looked as though I was to be more of a warden than a healthcare administrator!

The scope of the work involved providing substance abuse treatment services within a residential setting to adjudicated male adolescents within the Georgia Department of Juvenile Justice system (translation: incarceration and treatment for angry, addicted, male, teenage criminals). I felt comfortable only with two of those seven descriptive words—"treatment" and "addicted." This was going to be a problem.

I was immediately placed alongside the human resources department personnel who were hiring the remaining staff for this position. As a newcomer to this 25-year-old company, I had a lot to learn about the organizational culture, values and methods. This was a far cry from the polished hallways of public sector treatment with its overly professionalized, competitive and impersonal milieu. These folks were just one step away from a summer camp mentality. What they lacked in sophistication, however, they compensated for through passion and interpersonal relationships. They loved kids and held to very high standards for proper client care and growth.

I, on the other hand, had to overcome a couple of obstacles: my distaste for both teenagers and interpersonal relationships within the workplace. Still I was attracted to the opportunity to run a program and shoulder the responsibility of a startup operation. When we finished the hiring process there were 50 people under my supervision.

With just three weeks of in-service training, we "took delivery" of 30 young men into the new program. This rapid transition created numerous problems for the untested staff and protocols. By the second week we had already quelled three potential riots, managed one major escape and thwarted two more. By the end of week three I had personally assisted in numerous physical restraints and behavioral interventions; wrestled with insubordination and challenged apathy in most of the staff; been on the local news once (yes, four kids have escaped and, no, you don't need to hide your daughters); and responded to an actual riot at 2:00 a.m. I was done in—this was much more than I'd bargained for. What was I thinking, and where was God in all of this?

Once we had settled things down that evening, I gave my boss a verbal notice of resignation. She graciously followed me to the car, patted me on the shoulder and told me to take the next day off. Her counsel: "Think through your concerns now—you're going to be good at this."

I spent the next day searching the want ads. We had already relocated the family; the kids were adjusting to new schools. We were a three-hour drive from friends and our recovery network. My head was swirling. How to regroup from this disaster of a choice? I believe that I chatted with my boss later on that day. She was an unusually patient and persuasive woman—a seasoned leader with a knack for motivating people and instilling loyalty. By late evening I had recommitted to the decision to work for this company.

And I've never looked back . . .

The next three years brought success, accomplishment and promotion to my career. I was given supervision of an additional treatment program in North Carolina. With over 30 facilities in nine states, the opportunity to grow with this company increased. I brought the new assignment to a successful level of performance and began to solidify a reputation for being an effective troubleshooter and problem-solver.

Had I walked away from this challenge I would have missed a huge opportunity to grow and, ultimately, succeed. Opposition and setbacks seem to ultimately be part of the equation in terms of God's method of cultivating our spiritual maturity. Not that He necessarily creates these obstacles, but most certainly He uses them to our betterment. Learning to trust, subordinating personal hurts and fears, cultivating patience and resolving the deep wounds of our hearts all seem to be embedded in these lessons. If I'd chosen to run from this, I'd have missed out on an entire curriculum of essential life training. How many times have I sold myself short by running, or avoiding, life's sometimes painful lessons?

I was promoted to regional director of operations and given oversight of four programs—two in Georgia, one in North Carolina and one in Tennessee. On occasion I also assisted with a facility in Idaho. I could live where I wanted, as long as there was easy access to an airport and an interstate.

During this two-year season of growth and success we felt pulled to move back to Charleston, South Carolina, and rejoin our church. This was a highly disruptive decision and one that I'm not entirely certain was from God. We had by this point formed community in our relocation, and the kids were settling in well with their new school and friends. Still, I was at first intrigued and then obsessed with returning home.

I have this inherent, or learned, capacity to rationalize almost anything. This was most evident and destructive in my active addiction, but it still held sway in the immature places of my heart. As hard as I work to live from a place of transparency and pure motivation, I can formulate the most extravagant and improbable schemes and bring them to reality.

I've always thought that our liabilities and assets run on a continuum of sorts. Our challenge is to bring them into balance. My imagination is a wonderful gift . . . when used in conjunction with God's will. Left to my own devices, though, it can too easily be a source of chaos and a weapon of my spiritual enemy. From this all sorts of irrational fears, misperceptions, grandiosity and impulsivities are formulated.

When it comes to hearing from God, it's relatively easy for me to insert my own agenda. Partial truth supports this mindset. When I thought "*It would be good to get back to Charleston and worship with people we know. We have something to offer and can help those with addiction problems. We have grown so much since we were last there.*" There was some measure of truth in these rationalizations. But then I started to visualize all of the affirmation that would follow our welcome return to the "lost" congregation. People would be enlightened, souls would be saved, and the senior pastor would acknowledge my accomplishments during the three services next weekend. I would be on stage and ever humble in my response. I'd be known, respected and sought out.

HONK! I was startled in my reverie by the intrusive blaring of a car horn. Sitting in traffic, I was awakened by the sound of the impatient driver in the truck behind me (I'd managed to daydream all of this through a single stoplight cycle).

When this momentum gets going, it can be very difficult to stop. The runaway train of my thoughts continually fuels my anticipation and obsession. I check in with God and look for all sorts of signs throughout the day to affirm my pre-formulated plans.

I call this "breaking orbit" with God. A frenzy of activity increases the centrifugal force of my actions and will. What may have begun as a combination of God's will and my cooperation shifts to self-determination and a running after Jeff's will. I spin out of the circumference of the circle of life in God and slip uncontrollably into the alternative orbit of my ego. Self-will run riot. I become irritable, driven and determined. Obsessed. I shift from invitation to demand. I force things to work out, manipulate wherever I can. It's ugly and unfair when I drag others into this.

This was the mindset under which I was living when I made the decision to return to Charleston. In spite of my self-will, God was patient. I didn't at the time anticipate the full implications of God's working out all things for our/my good (paraphrase of Romans 8:28). Some tough lessons lay ahead.

Reflection Questions

Part of this chapter discusses encountering obstacles/defeat and discerning God's will in the face of opposition and confusion.

1. In what experience in your life have you encountered failure?
2. How did you manage these situations?
3. What, if anything, might you have done differently?
4. What resources would you need, or what kind of assistance from God, to do something differently?

18

ALL HELL BREAKS LOOSE

Thursday January 13, 2009

A US Airways jet landed in the Hudson River near Manhattan Thursday afternoon, plunging its 158 crew and passengers, including one infant, into freezing waters after apparently hitting a flock of geese. Miraculously, everyone aboard was able to escape, thanks to an incredible job **by pilot Chesley "Sully" Sullenberger** of Danville, Calif., who some witnesses said made a "three-point" landing on the water. "It would appear that the pilot did a masterful job of landing the plane in the river and making sure everyone got out," said Mayor Michael Bloomberg after the crash.

(excerpt from http://www.nbcnewyork.com/news/archive/Plane-Crashes-in-Hudson-River.html)

Coming back to Charleston was like landing a distressed aircraft. Encountering severe "turbulence" in various forms, we spent the next two years trying to salvage our faith, our hearts and even our sanity. Having entered into our personal *valley of the shadow of death*, we endured a season of pronounced suffering.

I briefly recount the specific events:
1. A family relative physically assaults our adolescent daughter.
2. Same family member physically and verbally assaults my wife.
3. The ensuing family and criminal court proceedings create tension, stress, chaos and vulnerability.
4. Financial stress related to the move and carrying the burden of two houses.
5. Conflict in church.
6. Abandonment by family members.
7. Disillusionment with the Christians with whom I'd been meeting.
8. Recurrent anxiety/panic attacks.

Indeed. My journal entry from eight months later recounts: "Since we moved here: Robin [my wife] assaulted, Sara [daughter] beaten, court ordeals and cost, tenant [House in Aiken we left behind] moved out without notice, HVAC broke in Aiken house, my truck was keyed, two cats mysteriously died."

Not surprisingly, I began to waver on our decision to come back to Charleston. Perhaps I had jumped the gun, taken matters into my own hands. The guilt and self-condemnation were excruciating. I was second-guessing everything. I resumed patterns of self-defeating behaviors I had long since put behind me—overspending, pornography, daydreaming about a way out. I was oversensitive and argumentative, feeling ill equipped to handle the multiple obstacles that appeared to be bombarding me. There seemed to be little support, and every social interaction served to exacerbate my pervasive feelings of abandonment and disappointment. I was a victim in my thinking, and no relief seemed forthcoming.

The ordeal constituted a spiritual and mental tug-of-war. The battles and conflict seemed to continually rise in intensity, and the ever-escalating stress was being driven both internally and externally. Almost incessantly I felt out of place in terms of where I was, who I was and what I was doing.

Still I held on to my faith and desire to follow God's will. I continued to practice the spiritual disciplines of devotion, tithing, repentance, prayer and worship. My self-soothing coping strategies were sporadic but quickly led to an increased determination to manage my shortcomings in a more beneficial and healthy manner.

In hindsight (isn't it always easier to interpret a situation from the vantage point of chronological distance?) I can pinpoint some key, spiritually developmental challenges and tests from this season. Max Lucado, contemporary Christian author and pastor, addresses this issue in one of his many books I have been privileged to read. He recounts a story of him and his family moving to Brazil in response to God's call on their lives. The reaction to their encounter with obstacles and conflict was predictable: had they made a mistake? A deeper revelation unfolded—the exposure of a false belief, critical to his growing faith: didn't following God's will mean that *things would go well, smoothly*? This author reaches the conclusion that, instead, we may count on *opposition* in the face of living obediently under God. Hell and high water *will* come!

Whoa, here was a new one. I was feeling the same way!! My orientation for discerning God's will in my life had been based upon how smoothly things began to unfold and move along under the momentum of my efforts. This would work itself out in either of two ways:

1. Self-determination: This simplistic approach required that I add some of my own expectation and bias to the mix. If, for example, I was "supposed to get that job," I first needed to visualize landing it. If this "felt good," I would apply and

"see what happens." If that led to an interview, this could be interpreted as "shaping up" with the direction of God's will. Otherwise, why had the process developed this far? An offer was firm validation that this must be the next move God has for me. If initiation was met with any resistance, I would quit. More of that unconscious self-determination in action.

2. God's invitation: This complex approach requires the discipline of self-restraint—not forcing opportunities but allowing them to come my way. A mental strategy of remaining emotionally balanced is also required. I have to reduce my imaginative projecting as well—must keep myself grounded enough to be present in the current events without forecasting how it will all work out. I can reasonably expect both opposition and risk. Faith bridges the summons. The questions always follow: "Is this your will, God?" "What am I to do here, now, in this circumstance?"

There are so many variables in this, which is precisely why it is essential to learn to hear God speak. The chaos that was involved in this season of my life served to bring maturity, albeit painfully, to the methods I would use to both hear and respond to God's direction in my life—refinement through the fires of tribulation, fear and confusion.

It was toward the end of this period that I read a book that brought clarity to where we had been, what we had suffered and what we could expect from that point. Our church started a sermon series based on the book *Waking the Dead* by John Eldredge. This study changed the entire trajectory of my spirituality and opened doors to a new life characterized by breakthrough, freedom and fulfillment.

And here's the interesting part, the summation of where this all comes together as a bridge, the lead-in to the turning point of the next chapter. Had we *not* moved back to Charleston (or had we left prematurely), we would *not* have met a certain couple over a casual dinner. This meeting led to a conversation about children's ministry and their behavioral health needs, along with a recommendation for us to visit a model program the couple knew of in Mars Hill, North Carolina. This would prove to be a critical turn of events for our lives, our spiritual formation, our careers and our eventual entry as a couple into vocational ministry. It was, unexpectedly, a divine appointment orchestrated by an intentional and faithful God.

Reflection Questions

This chapter opens with a news story about an airplane's crash landing—a metaphor for encountering overt opposition in following God's will. The author describes using poor coping strategies and reliance upon escapism in an effort to manage stress and goes on to make a comparison between reacting to life through self-determination and responding to it by accepting God's invitation.

1. When you try to "do the right thing," what kinds of problems do you sometimes encounter? Please elaborate.
2. Might God allow us to endure opposition when we are trying to do His will? If yes, why might this be?

19

SEARCHING FOR HOME

Tie me up and hold me down,
Bury my feet down in the ground,
Claim my name from the lost and found
And, let me believe this is where I belong . . .
—James Taylor, "Traveling Star," from his album *October Road*, 2004

The Appalachian Mountains were formed in the remote past by the collision of two Continental crusts. During such mountain building huge sheets of rock are pushed over each other. A rock layer called the Blue Ridge Thrust Sheet was moved over 60 miles to cover what is now Grandfather Mountain.

These mountains were once much higher (10 times as high!) than they are today. Erosion over hundreds of millions of years has carried away most of the rocks to form thick layers of sediment all across the Piedmont and Coastal Plain and in the Atlantic Ocean.

(http://www.grandfather.com/conservation_interpretation/geology.php)

I've always loved the mountains. As a child I had the opportunity to attend a couple of summer camps in that area. I'll never forget how deeply I was affected by this experience. The cool mountain lake, rolling terrain, misty morning dew and sweet smell of mountain laurel etched a vision for what I would later know as "my happy place."

There was an awe-inspiring peace about this venue. Every time I visited I found myself staring off toward some distant mountain—seemingly waiting to hear something. Was I asking a question, or was one being asked of me? A reverent "pondering" always seemed to captivate my thoughts—some existential longing in my soul.

Maybe I sensed the spirituality of beauty. The mind and heart long for this—a tangible yet ethereal connection to the Creator of everything. You feel as though all of this has "just happened" and that the artist has slipped away, satisfied with the finishing touches, only moments before you arrived. The stillness is deafening, a tranquility embedded in the surrounding mountain air. Sunshine seems to radiate love, and a mist shrouds the glory of majestic beauty. Already at a young age my heart sensed rest and belonging in this place. Some, I believe, are designed for the beach and others destined for the desert, but my native element seems to be these ancient remnants of original mountaintop glory.

The solace of the quiet life can be discovered in rural settings, and mountains in particular have a way of creating physical distance from one's neighbor. The area northwest of Asheville is even more defining. The steepness of the terrain lends itself to larger spaces between buildings. You need flat space for structures, and this almost always requires engineering and heavy equipment to accomplish.

All of the frustrations, emotional pain and exhaustion of the previous two years seemed to dissipate with the notion of moving to North Carolina. I had no problem leaving my childhood home in the rearview of the moving truck, as the emotional accumulation of memories, conflicts and struggles had been a huge disappointment. I needed to heal from the incessant assaults on my soul.

I visited Mars Hill, North Carolina, to visit a local Christian ministry and left convinced of my mission to return—permanently. We eventually found a six-acre parcel at the top of a ridgeline that would serve as the ideal place to build a log home. After a difficult effort on my part to persuade our children, my employer and my wife that this was a good idea, we left Charleston in June 2004 to begin a new phase of life in the mountains.

It was during this time that I sensed a desire to find community at a deeper level. Several years of traveling had cemented the realization that I had never really belonged anywhere, at least not in a civic sense. I hadn't been able to make commitments to many activities because of my frequent work-related absences. I had become a visitor in my own town. Moving to the mountain community I wanted to be a part of something, to *know* and *be known*, build relationships, accomplish community-minded objectives, establish a name and sink roots.

During the course of this transition I happened upon an advertisement for an executive director position. The job description dovetailed with my résumé and offered an opportunity to meet the criteria of community I had begun to yearn for. The scope of this company's outreach covered eight counties, and it managed approximately $50 million in annual revenue. Having previously managed a program within the North Carolina mental health system, I was already aware of some of the technical aspects of this particular organization. The rest could be learned. With nothing to lose, I tossed in my résumé.

The next four months (did you know an interview process could last that long?) were a whirlwind of conversations and interactions. Apparently a lot of people thought as I did about this job and this location—a whopping 156 candidates all told. At each interval/stage I would submit my best answers to the inquiries, ranging from phone interviews to a videotaped presentation. And after each such event I would later find myself invited to participate in the next round. And so it went, from April through June.

At one point in this rather daunting process I was informed by email that I hadn't been passed along to the next level. While somewhat surprised at this stage and mildly disappointed, I shrugged this off and focused on what was in front of me. However, a further communication the next morning revealed this to have been an error. I was invited to participate in the final round, along with only three other candidates. This entailed a three-day weekend of further interviews; dinner with the governing board; a public forum (*really?*); and, finally, a meeting with the organization's management team.

The whirlwind of activity thrust me into contact with some of the area's predominant leaders. Handshakes and introductions led to further inquiry and examination into my competency and viability as a leader. It was a long and exhausting weekend, but I felt confident of a solid performance. After the final meeting the head of the search committee personally escorted me to my car and asked about my salary requirements. I knew I had the job!

With promises that I would hear something by the following week, I continued to daydream about my new position. I would do great things here and make good money doing it. Five years postgraduate from my master's degree would have me well ahead of my cohorts from the university. I would be embedded in the community and hold the profile of a community leader. Newspaper interviews would soon follow.

When the phone didn't ring by the following Friday, I took the initiative to investigate. The search committee chairman briefly and officially informed that I had come close but that the board's vote had not been unanimous. (I had no idea that the 19-member board had to come through with a unanimous decision—what could be the odds of that happening?!). In the end they had opted to stay with their incumbent. The entire search process had evidently taken place on the basis of a divisive desire on the part of some to fire this guy and bring in a fresh face. All of that effort, not to mention expense, to maintain the status quo! You just have to love bureaucratic logic!

The disappointment settled in throughout the weekend. By Sunday I was thoroughly depressed, surprised that this process had taken such a hold on my desires. I struggled with a sense both of rejection and of failure. What had I done wrong? Why had all of this gone so far, only to end in defeat? Why had I latched on so strongly to this possibility? Recurring questions from prior experiences haunted my awareness.

By midweek I was emotionally moving on but mentally still struggling to figure something out. Trouble was, I just couldn't pinpoint what. There was some nagging, back-of-mind of question I couldn't bring to the surface, not to mention some elusive declarative statement trying to emerge from the depths of my subconscious. I felt preoccupied by some compulsion rising within me that needed to be acted upon.

The formation of October Road Incorporated, a concept that would develop into a multi-million dollar company, emerged as an idea at precisely 3:00 a.m. on Thursday, July 29, 2004. The culmination of disappointment, confusion and searching abruptly woke me in the early morning hours. To my surprise and exhilaration, I had reached the conclusion "I can do this myself!" With this came a compulsion to go downstairs (my office was in the garage-basement) and write all of this down.

A flurry of thoughts and ideas began surfacing in my conscious mind. I could hardly keep my thoughts together as I frantically typed away at the Word document freshly opened on my laptop. As the sun rose that morning and I came up for air, I satisfied myself that I had typed out the mission, vision, name and values of the company I knew I could found and build. The best of everything I had encountered in my career would come to focus within this new entity.

The first value that came to mind was *gratitude*.

We are grateful for the gift of life, the challenges we face and the opportunity to fulfill our purpose through the use of our God given gifts, uniquely provided to us for the fulfillment of His glory.

God was in this and I knew it, felt it. All of this was His idea. My ego began to soften from the blow of rejection and failure I had so recently experienced. Clearly I had projected my expectations of success and need for validation into the effort to be selected. I had been working to persuade the selection board to like me and invite me in to their mission, to become a part of something big and good. This, at bottom, was the source of my disappointment. Ironically, the whole prolonged production had prepared me to learn and apply all I needed in order to open and operate a behavioral healthcare company in the community.

I constructed an action plan to pursue the development of this concept over the course of the next two years. This included interviewing current stakeholders (providers of services, leaders, payors and regulatory officials), researching the market and completing some required training to enhance my professional credentials.

I continued to work at my corporate job, traveling frequently, interspersed with a few days at the home office. During this two-year period an interim concept materialized in my mind, on the impetus of which I opened a martial arts training school and fitness center. Part of my journey to that point included six years of martial arts training, along with the acquisition of a black belt and instructor certification. Teaching was a natural desire and gift of mine, blending well with my entrepreneurial drive. This connection also helped integrate our family into the small and tight mountain community. I developed a business plan and approached the local banks for monetary assistance, aka, "I needed a loan."

A parenthetical word about customer service:

"U.S. firms spent about $156 billion on employee learning in 2011, the most recent data available, according to the American Society for Training and Development." (*The Wall Street Journal*, US Edition. October 26, 2012)

156 billion dollars! That's enough money to fund the State of South Carolina's budget needs for more than 30 years! Having been employed within various professional organizations for over two decades, I can accurately declare that a significant portion of that referenced $156 billion is directed toward some form of customer service training. Let's conjecture, conservatively, that this is 5%, or approximately $8 billion.

All of this effort and cost are designed to attract and retain customers. Because it costs more to acquire than to keep customers, retention is the big goal here. No customer retention, no business. It's that simple.

Customer service is like common sense—it isn't all that common; nor is it complicated. Simply stated, it has a biblical ring: treat other people in the same way you want to be treated. Whatever it is you do, do it well and do it courteously. Be reliable—do what you say you will. Call people back and acknowledge that you've heard from them. Give assurance that you care and that their business is important to you. Let them know they matter. When you make a mistake (and you will), own up to it. Listen well. Solve people's problems.

I dropped off my business plan at two different banking institutions, both well-known, reputable international corporations. You can bet they put the big bucks into customer service. This is a highly competitive industry.

To simplify the story, we'll call the first institution "Bank A." I made an appointment with the loan officer, briefly reviewed my plan, provided him with a 10-page, professional-grade document and made sure he had all of my contact information. He never called back, in spite of my numerous attempts to follow up. No acknowledgement of my plan, no "thanks but no thanks"—no response, period. Incidentally, this bank is the one with which I had done my personal banking for the previous 10 years.

"Bank B" was, and is, BB&T—Branch Banking and Trust. I'd had no prior relationship with this institution but followed the same protocol. I received a phone call within two days with a request to meet with me. The loan officer asked whether she could bring her vice president with her and whether they could drive out to the proposed business location. They were intrigued enough to check the location; meet with me; and gather details about our plans, intentions and needs. We signed a small business loan for $45,000 within the month.

I've been a highly satisfied customer of BB&T since November 2005. They've been an ally for both my personal and my corporate needs. Over the years I've run millions of dollars through their institution. A large part of my business success was and is tied to our banking relationship.

Allow me to clarify that I've received no compensation from them or anyone else for this part of my narrative. I'm simply providing a pertinent example of how customer service can make or break a business relationship. How many times a day does this come into play throughout the course of our routine business dealings? With regard to our governmental services? Our churches and nonprofits? It can make all the difference in success or failure.

Over the course of 18 months our little karate school grew from three students to sixty. We invested effort, time and money (thanks, BB&T) into acquiring and modifying a vacant building. This experience trained us in the finer details of personalizing and applying a business plan.

It's one thing to come into an opportunity and manage someone else's money. There is in this relationship a buffer, a sense of immunity, no matter how conscientious one may be, regarding the possibility of failure. There are training wheels in place, or a safety net, if you will. When working for a corporate entity I once made a budget error in the form of a $180,000 projection shortfall. While I felt bad about it, this didn't have the same effect as a $500 shortfall on my own weekly cash receipts. Say what you want about being a conscientious and caring employee, but it gets downright personal when it's your money on the line.

Riding the ups and downs of this small business endeavor provided me with the tolerance to handle cash flow challenges. Red isn't the color you want to see in your budget reports. We had a good plan, but efficiency and employee reliability were impeding our ability to hold steady at the bottom line. Still, we were successful in the overall effort. Lessons were learned at many levels—lessons that would become invaluable for the next endeavor—opening a behavioral healthcare company.

Reflection Questions

The author describes an opportunity to live and work in the mountains of North Carolina, as well as encountering a disappointment in the area of a hoped for career opportunity and how this led to the founding and formation of a successful business venture. He also provides facts and commentary on the aspects of excellent customer service and relates how this is fundamental to success in both life and business.

1. How do you feel when you read stories of failure or rejection turned into success?
2. When this happens, do you attribute the ultimate success to self-determination or self-confidence, or do you feel there's more involved? Please explain.
3. What has been your experience in terms of failure and success?
4. Identify examples of both good and bad customer service you've encountered in the past year. What happened?

5. Why do you think some companies are better at this than others? What role do individual employees play in terms of overall quality?
6. What sort of customer are you? If you were working on the other side of the counter from yourself, what would be your impressions of the customer?

20

LAUNCHING THE NEXT PHASE

In the summer of 2006 I realized that I was bored. Busy, but bored—unfulfilled, really. Mornings spent in quiet reflection revealed that I had worked myself out of a job. My tenure with my current employer had reached seven years, the longest I had stayed with anyone. I provided administrative oversight to five programs in three states. The local administrators were doing a fine job in making my life easy. Most of my visits were more of an intrusion than a benefit.

I felt unchallenged. The efforts toward stabilizing and growing the programs and staff had paid off. Everything was working well. I remember telling my wife that I felt as though I were just taking the company's money, not really earning it.

The draw to engage in community was being satisfied by the fitness and martial arts business. But I was still traveling. I made a few minor attempts to apply for some other local management jobs but never landed a serious interview. Seemed that if I were going to do anything different, it would require that I activate the plan I had envisioned two years earlier.

Open a counseling business. Probably the dream of many therapists. You get good at something and at some point you start figuring you can do it better under your own volition and control. All of the implied limitations of "working for the man" seem escalated in light of the idea that you can run your own enterprise. Sometimes that's true; most of the time it isn't. Owning a successful business is much more than doing whatever your vocation is. Turning this into a reality is a matter of commitment, determination and perseverance mixed with just the right amount of naiveté and idealism.

I opened up the business plan that had been developing over the past two years. Where to start? A brief look at finances revealed that whatever I did I would only have three months to begin turning a profit—not a good prospect since startup businesses typically lose money through the first three years. Still, I felt as though I were heading in the right direction. Prayer, conversation with others and a license as a substance abuse therapist seemed to hold promise that it was time to launch out on my own. My accountant, ever the realist, thought otherwise. "You have a mortgage, two car payments, a current business held by a loan, and two children heading to college. Don't be silly—wait three years and ease into it."

He was right. I had every reason financially to stay put. Stock options, control over my schedule, an easy management job, good pay, health insurance, seniority and job security. Play it safe—be responsible. This was good counsel. It just wasn't what God had in mind; the timing of this move would later prove to be critical and essential to our success.

I am not advocating for foolishness and reckless abandon. In decisions regarding career, education and family—any major life choices—we have responsibilities and must take into account the needs and stakes of others. Walking a tightrope can be exhilarating, but both victory and defeat lie waiting within the small steps it takes to launch the adventure. Once you're out there feeling your way across that taut rope you can't turn back. Going forward is the only way safely through the passage.

But God had made it clear to me that this was the time. I knew this deep within my soul. I had spent literally hours on that cabin porch, not idle but surrendering my agenda and waiting, listening, perceiving. My vantage point started with discontent and moved toward possibility, invitation and, finally, calling. An old saying has it that "where God leads, He will provide." I had built up a good deal of experience in God's provision over the years. Even in my foolishness and immaturity He had been infinitely gracious. Never holding back. I've always had what I needed through His faithfulness.

More than that, I was responding in obedience. Taking a risk means not knowing exactly how things will all work out. God is faithful in what He will do, but my experience revealed that he had a propensity for waiting till the last minute before coming through. Sometimes, when failure seemed to loom as a certainty and I was convinced beyond doubt that some catastrophic show stopper was about to block my way, God, niftily and without fanfare, changed the outcome.

I made the decision to leave my employer and launch out on my own. I would provide substance abuse counseling services to drunk driving offenders—often a gateway opportunity to engage people in treatment at an early intervention stage. Besides, this was to be a cash-only business—allowing me to avoid the complications of third-party insurance or contracting with the quasi-governmental local management entity. It would be just me and the clients; if it got busy enough I'd hire a part-time therapist on contract.

I attended a weeklong seminar on serving and treating offenders under the DWI laws in North Carolina. Holding a substance abuse license gave me an advantage, as this higher level credential afforded opportunity to differentiate my service line. I spent part of the class time projecting numbers on a scribble pad, estimating revenue and expenses for the new business venture. It looked feasible . . . on paper anyway.

I confirmed the plans with my wife. I can't say enough how great a life partner she has been to me. Her enthusiastic support and confidence in my ability to succeed have served to bring me the essential courage needed to take risks like this. With her affirmation I notified my employer that I would be leaving. We worked out an agreement for a 60-day transition. I would then have three weeks of paid leave, followed by a month of leave payout. Add to that a retirement account cash-out, and I would have about thirteen weeks to make a go of it.

On August 15, 2006, seven years to the day of my previous hire, I left the safety of the corporate world and jumped feet first into the shark-infested waters of private enterprise. I was to be my own boss—the epitome of the American dream.

Reflection Questions

This chapter includes a narrative and discussion on the subject of evaluating and taking risks in life and business. It also addresses the aspect of faith, especially in terms of applying it under genuine risk.

1. What did you think about the author's leaving a stable job and venturing out into his own—in some sense unknown, despite careful planning—business?
2. Do you believe that God may call you out of your comfort zone to do something risky? Has He upon occasion already done so? If so, what has this looked like in your life?
3. There's a difference between being confused about God's will and being obedient to His will. Has there been a time in your life when you felt as though God were, or might be, calling you to do something and you felt hesitant, reluctant or downright rebellious? Please elaborate.

21

OUT THE GATE

The original business plan showed an optimistic projected annual income of $240,000. Don't get prematurely excited here—planned-for expenses came in at around $200,000, leaving a net of $40,000 for year one. This wasn't only half my recent salary but was wholly contingent upon whether the clients would show up. And whether they'd pay their bills . . . *if* I was still open for business.

This is precisely the point at which many dreams are kept from becoming reality: "*I looked at the plan yet again, objectively, and there's just no way I can do it.*" Whether it's going back to school, trying a new hobby, starting a new life routine (eating, exercise, spirituality) or even writing a book (who wants to read *my* story?), we can be stalled before we get out of the gate. Within the razor sharp timelines of track and field, you can beat another runner by causing them to hesitate. Timing out of the gate is critical to building momentum and optimum performance. A bad start will kill an otherwise stellar performance and, with it, any opportunity for victory.

When God invites us into more freedom, more life, the process is almost always disruptive. There's never a perfect time to do anything. There are always obstacles. Desire and dream-to-reality entail overcoming the limitations and uncertainties reality brings. Time, schedule, money, inconvenience. Are you ready to pay the cost for success, for victory? Because it *will* come with a price. Are you willing to endure discomfort, anxiety, uncertainty? With God all things are possible. He loves us as we are but isn't willing to leave us that way. He calls us out to take risks, to become more than we already are—perhaps we could think of this as more *of* the positive things we already are—by relying on Him for what we can be. This is what separates what *could* have been from what *can* be—and, ultimately, what *will* be and later *is*.

We need something to bridge the gap between our hesitation and the confidence to move out of our comfort zone. We need faith, but how do we acquire it?

Consider looking backward. An honest survey of our lives will reveal to us those areas in which God has been faithful. I'm aware that many of my readers may balk at this. A background filled with a long assault upon a broken heart can be a painful well from which to draw. But look more closely.

In his Narnia series C. S. Lewis continues with his gospel allegory begun in *The Horse and His Boy*. In one particular scene the boy Shasta has been left behind from his company of friends and allies. As he travels on alone he begins to feel sorry for himself because of all the terrible misfortunes he has had to endure. In the midst of his confusion and emptiness Aslan (a.k.a. Jesus / the Holy Spirit) shows up. As the travel wears on and his mind is consumed with consuming regret and self pity, he becomes frighteningly aware that some unseen *thing* has been following him. He struggles to raise the courage to ask and reluctantly pleads for the thing to go away. Let's pick up the story there:

"Who are you?" he said, barely above a whisper.

"One who has waited long for you to speak," said the Thing. Its voice was not loud, but very large and deep.

"Are you—are you a giant?" asked Shasta.

"You might call me a giant," said the Large Voice. "But I am not like the creatures you call giants."

"I can't see you at all," said Shasta, after staring very hard. Then (for an even more terrible idea had come into his head) he said, almost in a scream, "You're not—not something dead, are you? Oh please—please do go away. What harm have I ever done you? Oh, I am the unluckiest person in the whole world."

Once more he felt the warm breath of the Thing on his hand and face. "There," it said, "that is not the breath of a ghost. Tell me your sorrows."

Shasta was a little reassured by the breath: so he told how he had never known his real father or mother and had been brought up sternly by the fisherman. And then he told the story of his escape and how they were chased by lions and forced to swim for their lives; and of all their dangers in Tashbaan and about his night among the Tombs and how the beasts howled at him out of the desert. And he told about the heat and thirst of their desert journey and how they were almost at their goal when another lion chased them and wounded Aravis. And also, how very long it was since he'd had anything to eat.

"I do not call you unfortunate," said the Large Voice.

"Don't you think it was bad luck to meet so many lions?" said Shasta.

"There was only one lion," said the Voice.

"What on earth do you mean? I've just told you there were at least two lions the first night, and—"

"There was only one, but he was swift of foot."

"How do you know?"

"I was the lion."

And as Shasta gaped with open mouth and said nothing, the Voice continued. "I was the lion who forced you to join with Aravis. I was the cat who comforted you among the houses of the dead. I was the lion who drove the jackals from you as you slept. I was the lion who gave the Horses the new strength of fear for the last mile so that you should reach King Lune in time. And I was the lion you do not remember who pushed the boat in which you lay, a child near death, so that it came to shore where a man sat, wakeful at midnight, to receive you."

"Then it was you who wounded Aravis?"

"It was I."

"But what for?"

"Child," said the Voice, "I am telling you your story, not hers. I tell no one any story but his own."

A retrospective assessment of our lives will reveal that God has always been with us and for us. Don't get lost in the "why" of events—some of that detail may come to light later on. Stay here, in the "now" assurance that He'll never remove His hand from you, even when circumstances would suggest otherwise. Faith will arise in the process of discerning the truth. Look for that for which you can be grateful, and you'll hone in on those areas in which

God has been most evidently faithful. If He was before, He will be again. Ask Him to show you this; then bask in the peace He brings.

It's *that* assurance, *that* faith that brings confidence. Enough confidence *to enable you to take risks!* As is evident from my story, I've taken risks in my life over and over again. The first was to let go of alcohol and search beyond it for a new meaning to life. From there on the calculated risks only escalated—marriage, school and career with all their stages and nuances. Moving, staying put and trying new things. Exploring life, while fully expecting and believing that even in failure (however that may be defined) I'd be okay. If I make the effort, the outcome will always be up to God, no matter where it eventually lands.

Reflection Questions

A backward glance at the chapter calls to mind commentary on moving from dreams to reality; using experience as a reassurance for trusting God; focusing the lens of interpretation; pragmatic application in acquiring faith; and the C. S. Lewis extract from *A Horse and His Boy*.

1. Is there a dream or plan in your life over which you've hesitated to act out of fear or uncertainty?
2. List three examples from your life of times when you were certain God had come through for you?
3. What would it take for you to move toward fulfillment of your dream or plan in life? What's holding you back? What do you feel a need to hear, see or know from God?
4. Can you identify ways in which some of the painful experiences in your life have been arranged for your good or used by God for your own or others' benefit? Elaborate on the ramifications.

22

TIMING IS EVERYTHING

Launching an enterprise, or any plan for that matter, requires a keen sense of timing. Market factors such as demand, competition, product differentiation (ways in which my product is unique from that of my competitors) all play a role in the probable success or failure of the plan. I had all of this clearly in mind when I ventured into opening my own business. However, as a friend of mine likes to quip, "I'm glad I'm lucky rather than smart."

The interim period between planning and implementation involved finding a location and developing the operating policies and procedures. Regulation is intense in the behavioral health field, especially when public funding applies. All of the systems, plans and procedures had to be in place in advance of any licensing. So the 60 or so days were filled with the mundane but necessary: hours upon hours in local coffee shops, pounding away at a laptop; writing plans and procedures representing a corporate entity that had yet to pay its first electric bill.

I acquired a leased space while out buying gift certificates for some of our gym employees. Dressed in shorts and flip-flops, I more resembled a tourist than a businessman when I met the landlord. An impromptu stop and inquiry led to this unplanned discussion, and I found myself struggling to portray some level of credibility.

After I had stammered something about needing space for my new, but not yet established, enterprise, he asked what I could pay for the space. I tossed out a rough educated guess based upon other properties I had seen (in much worse location and condition). He accepted my business card and said he would get back with me. That night a contract was on my fax machine for 2,000 square feet of medical office space, in a prime location at a fraction of the market price. Unbelievable.

It was during this interim period that I was also approached by a manager from a local provider of mental health services. Since I knew him within another social context, he was aware that I was opening a small business. Seems that there were some significant concerns about the ethical behavior of his organization's superior—something about a proclivity toward sleeping with the clients! This, along with some executive fiscal mischief, had led him, along with 13 of his coworkers, to consider leaving en masse. Torn as they were between moving out into their own venture or aligning with another provider, he asked on all of their behalf whether I would consider incorporating them into my business plan. A second meeting ironed out the agreement, including my requirement that they inform their current employer well in advance of their departure. This would provide him with ample time to accommodate the changes—a professional courtesy, but more importantly an issue of honesty and integrity.

The second concern was practice: the evident fact that I couldn't pay these folks. A 15-member team, including myself, would require a monthly payroll of $62,000! There would be no immediate way to manage that burden during the eternal space between the incurring of expenses and the beginning of revenue collections. Besides, we weren't even an official provider yet. We needed to be accredited and establish a contract with the local management entity. All of that could take several months.

But we pressed on. It was within this arrangement that October Road moved overnight from a one-man enterprise to, after all was said and done, a 20-member team. With the hiring of some support staff we rounded out our personnel and moved our efforts toward acquiring the necessary credentialing and firming up contractual arrangements.

And then it happened: the largest provider of substance abuse and mental health services in the region closed its doors abruptly, the victim of mental health reform. The mental health re-formation required governmental entities to shift toward a business model. The purpose was to raise the quality of care for clients (consumers could choose their provider) and manage the rising costs associated with treating mental health / substance abuse / developmental disabilities issues within the state system. Instead of divesting their services to private providers, many public sector agencies converted to nonprofit agencies and separated themselves from governmental ties. A stroke of the pen and some new paint on the walls and the organization became another entity overnight. Many, however, failed to change their practices, which is why reform had come about in the first place. When the business model (the paradigm of *earning* the income) replaced the public sector model (check is in the mail, regardless of what you've earned), it was only a matter of time before such a house of cards collapsed.

With this single event 10,000 clients and 750 employees flooded the market. And there we were, just as though our entree had all been planned. They never taught us this level of strategic accuracy in business school!

The next three months were marked by a flurry of activity, with our new company trying not to drown in the burgeoning requests for services. We provided services, all right, while holding on to the billing—not having yet received our contractual billing authority! Accounts receivables (they owe us money) looked great, but here was no cash to back up the rising expenses. By November we were in desperate need of money, and it appeared that it would likely be January before we could collect a dime. The banks weren't yet convinced, and I couldn't blame them. We needed help.

"Once I was young, and now I am old. Yet I have never seen the godly abandoned or their children begging for bread." (Psalm 37:25, NLT)

Since I entered into recovery I've never missed paying a bill or been without food, shelter or opportunity. Yet our bills were beginning to add up. The support staff had to be paid, as did the lights, cell phones and vendors for our office supplies.

I called an elderly woman I had met while teaching her grandson martial arts. She had been impressed with our school and values and had offered at the time to invest financially if we ever wanted to grow the gym. After several failed attempts to beg and borrow from other associates, I phoned her on a Monday evening and presented her with our current business plan, requesting an unspecified loan to help us get through the startup season. She asked me to meet with one of her adult sons and run it by him.

On Wednesday evening he came by our offices, and the pitch was made. Graphs and spreadsheets accompanied the presentation. His affect wasn't indicative of a response one way or the other; though polite, he seemed indifferent. We parted with the usual gestures, and he mentioned that he'd be in touch.

I needed to meet payroll by Friday but lacked the resources to do so. Paying one's staff must always be the highest priority. Building consideration, respect and reliability were essential to our reputation as a new company and core to our values. Clichéd as this may sound, we needed a miracle.

I arrived at the gym to teach the evening martial arts class on Thursday, at which time an unexpected check in the amount of $60,000 was handed to me by our new benefactor. This was accompanied by a small loan contract with fair terms and repayment conditions. We would make it through the season!

Our benefactor passed away just one month later due to chronic health problems. Timing is everything—on many levels. We have so little control over life's variables. I'm pleased to report that she was a devout Christian and that her eternal future was secure. God was there and she came through in our time of need, making all the difference for us.

How could we have planned for that?

Our first receivables check arrived in January 2007 in the amount of $120,000. We were finally beginning to gain some traction!

Reflection Questions

This chapter discusses business implications within the concept of decision making and timing. It relates specific examples of challenges and anxieties in operating a business, as well as miraculous provision of needs and attribution to God's guidance in orchestrating events, people and provision.

"Once I was young, and now I am old. Yet I have never seen the godly abandoned or their children begging for bread." (Psalm 37:25, NLT)

1. How do you respond to this verse from Psalm 37? Are you immediately skeptical, looking for the obvious exceptions to this principle of godly living, or are you flooded with gratitude for the practical truth of David's reflection in your own life? What reasoning and what emotion arise in your mind and heart?
2. Can you recall a time when you made a risky decision and things just seemed to line up for you? If so, why do you think this happened?
3. Do you believe that God will take the "time" and "effort" (if these human constructs are applicable to God!) to work out details for your benefit? Why or why not?

Application Exercise

Make a list of 10 things in your life for which you're grateful:

Moving beyond the obvious reality that God is in everything, what did God have to do with these things?

Does He have your best interest in mind? That is, does He really care about you? Please elaborate.

23

TIGER BY THE TAIL

"Be careful what you wish for,
'cause you just might get it all,
and then some you don't want."

—Chris Daughtry, *"Coming Home,"* 2007

We spent the rest of the year trying to keep up with demand and growth. Space issues, technology and human resource infrastructure, along with formation of our cultural identity, created competing priorities and challenges to be resolved with a limited amount of time. I was at the same time juggling the gym/martial arts business and managing family and recovery life.

We acquired additional space that effectively tripled our original office footprint. By November we were on target to break $1 million in revenue. We were also awarded the "Provider of the Year" designation by the local management entity. Our reputation was developing nicely with all of our stakeholders.

Cash flow remained a challenge, however. This isn't uncommon in healthcare, where receivables (the money people owe you) can take 45–60 days to reconcile (for you to get paid). Meanwhile, liabilities (bills you owe) come due rapidly within this cycle, making a cash cushion necessary to sustain the operation. Payroll is the biggest and most immediate cost driver. These cash outflows can cycle three times before a payment comes in to cover the costs.

I spent many a Friday afternoon hovering over the checkbook, fretting over the negative numbers that appeared after making good on payroll checks. I knew the money was out there, but we never knew exactly when it would come in. A typical example would develop as follows:

Since I served as the accounts payable officer (along with wearing many other hats), I would write checks every other Friday, corresponding with the biweekly payday. Anyone dropping by to chat would quickly be reminded that if they wanted to get paid they'd better keep moving! Bills and papers were invariably strewn about, my face buried in a ledger of activity, calculator in hand. By noon I would have everything sorted and written, the checkbook ledger reconciled, and be out the door to a recovery meeting to find some personal gratitude and sanity.

On one particular afternoon I left the office with the tense reality that we were $26,000 in the red (that's as in $0 - $26,000 = -$26,000). The payroll checks would be handed out that afternoon, and I had nowhere to acquire the funds. A highly creative and resourceful person, I'll have to admit that I was stumped by this dilemma. People needed their checks, and the company's young reputation hinged on every paid bill, every fulfilled promise. There was absolutely nowhere to turn for help. I gave the situation to God and did my best to release my worries within the confines of my meeting.

I returned to the office some time later to finish out the administrative duties of the week. I knew I had done all I could do and was mentally preparing for the fallout that would occur when checks started to bounce. I would lose employees, . . . and understandably so. We would teeter in our credibility and could easily slip into obscurity, losing all of the fragile relational capital we had acquired to date. The fall would be ugly and costly.

An envelope I hadn't noticed before my departure lay next to the office phone, a disruptive intruder upon my tidy desktop. My stomach always dropped when I encountered the unforeseen. Who was resigning now?

As I opened the envelope, the background of an official check highlighted the contents. It was a payment for a series rendered in the amount of $50,000—arriving two weeks early! A quick trip to deposit this, and our ledger was more than balanced! We had gone from red to black in a matter of four hours.

There were countless highs and lows of this kind. As I noted before, stepping out in faith is like walking a tightrope. It's at the same time both exhilarating and unnerving. You can't rehearse this in the laboratory of theory and speculation, behind a podium or in a church sanctuary for a service. This spiritual formation is cast within the fires and trials of daily life.

And God always comes through. He is with us and for us, coaching, encouraging and training. Calling us to be more than frail and fearsome creatures—to be bold kings and queens in His kingdom's manifestation here on Earth. To beckon in heaven's authority and reign in the freedom of a life first restored and then well lived. In hope, in promise, in assurance, with intimacy and relational dependency upon the One who was once known as a Jewish carpenter from Nazareth—the same One who died so we might live. His life resides within us now, so we can overcome the mundane and earthly and overwhelmingly demonstrate His glory and faithfulness in the common, yet overwhelming, needs of this world ... and of our lives.

We survived our first year in this fashion and had the attention of the community and stakeholders to show for it.

With Victory Comes Challenge

The year 2008 brought the most difficult and painful times of my tenure with October Road. Three major events played into the scenario:

1. The abrupt resignation of two key managers, their service teams and numerous customers poached from our client rosters.
2. The acquisition of a major substance abuse grant.
3. The death of my mother.

All three of these events rocked my foundational motivation of optimism and hope. Betrayal came in the form of a resignation on the parts of my friends and managers. They had been working on a business plan for months and were now going to launch it—right down the street from where they had asked to join me. The clandestine method of their planning, along with the aggressive behaviors that followed, served to fuel a deep injury within my soul. We lost over $100,000 in direct revenue within six months as a direct result of these actions. Replacement costs for staff and clients would double this. The expenditures of time, mental energy and emotion could be assigned no dollar figure. It was tough.

To counterbalance this exigency, we were fortunate to acquire a substance abuse expansion grant. This was a huge undertaking, but one about which I was most excited. The grant had both a residential component and a long-term funding source. We were able to design a comprehensive continuum of care that would prove highly effective in bringing deep healing and restoration to hundreds of men struggling with mental health and substance abuse issues.

During the design phase of this project my mother passed away. I had deeply loved and respected this woman and had wondered what I would do and how I would manage after she eventually passed. In my characteristic manner, I managed this loss compartmentally in terms of my task-oriented mind. While I grieved her passing briefly, I could attend to it only within the confines of a limited availability. But the reality is that this kind of life passage demands full attention; otherwise, what's left buried will inevitably rear its head again, demanding resolution. It would do just that in 2009.

In August 2008 (at age 46) I attended a significant and life-changing retreat known as Wild at Heart Boot Camp. Unlike many other men's retreats I had attended, this four-day experience immersed me in the larger story of the gospel. With unprecedented clarity the narrative and themes of the Trinity, evil, the fall of man, the heart of God as He pursues His lost creation, the provision of a Savior and the restoration of humanity were illustrated in deep and meaningful ways. This experience memorably reinforced the reality of who I was and what my role in this world and in this life were meant to be. My masculinity was validated, but the experience at the same time revealed the great chasm of brokenness that still lingered in my heart. Much more work would still be required, although I was infused with deep hope and desire.

I could site dozens of examples of the obstacles, challenges and miraculous outcomes through which I lived during this time frame. I offer these two years of opening and operating the company, along with what I was encountering in my daily life, as a reference point for how God walked with me in and through this unique season. But this combined experience marked for me another beginning, a tearing of my soul that would expose the deeper wounds, vows and spiritual traps that had accumulated and still resided around my heart.

Reflection Questions

The author recounts details of the challenges inherent in managing a rapidly growing business, while also revealing transparent reflections about his thoughts and fears. He describes and reflects on how these led to a season of testing and enhancing faith.

1. Starting a new job, becoming involved in a new relationship or going through any other significant lifestyle change can be both risky and exhilarating. Reflect on an example from your own life within the past five years (go back further if you need to).
2. Did you encounter a period of fear and anxiety or face some sort of problem after taking action on your decision? How did you handle that?
3. When this happens, do you:
    a. interpret this as a sign that you've made the wrong decision?
    b. change the plan or try to backtrack?
    c. dig in and hold to the commitment?
4. Do you have a support group, community or church group with whom you can process and share these experiences? If not, are you willing to affiliate with one? Why or why not?

24

MY DARK NIGHT OF SENSE

Seems like all I could see was the struggle
Haunted by ghosts that lived in my past
Bound up in shackles of all my failures
Wondering how long is this gonna last?
Then you look at this prisoner and say to me, son
Stop fighting a fight that's already been won
And I am redeemed. You set me free
So I'll shake off these heavy chains and wipe away every stain
I am redeemed . . .

—"Redeemed," by Big Daddy Weave,
from the album *Love Come to Life*, 2013

In 2009 I enrolled in a course for a Certificate of Christian Studies—an immersion into Christian doctrine. People have often asked me why I chose to attend seminary. A growing interest in returning to school, along with an intense desire to discover "why I believe what I believe" led me to the doors of Asbury Theological Seminary. I desperately needed to understand.

My friend Michael Thompson of Zoweh Ministries puts it like this: "I want to know why I believe, that what I believe is really real."

Yes—that's it in a nutshell! I had been pursued and found. Discovered in the tangled mess of alcoholism; drenched in sin and defiance; angry and afraid; a cornered, feral, wounded dog snarling at his rescuer. Jesus came and pulled me out of all this. He gave me a way back to God by circumventing the obstacles of organized religion. Through twelve-step recovery and the help of professionals and friends, I gained freedom and an increased desire to know Him.

Fast-forward 18 years. I have moved in and out of church life and read thousands of pages from good Christian authors. I have loved, sought out, worshiped, listened to and obeyed God. I've applied the principles of Christian living and have tasted the sweetness of healing and grace, time and again.

It's amazing that God is willing to stoop to come after us. He never changes, and we find either confusion or comfort in that fact—or maybe guilt . . . or conviction.

I find that I (like others) am a tangle of contradictions and compromises. I sustain this discordant mix on a platform of rationalizations and justifications. It's an endless cycle, a "fuel cell" of perpetual momentum that keeps me exasperatingly isolated from the truth. I avoid the implications of my limitations by anticipating what will be needed for each situation—preparing to avoid it altogether or at least prearranging for it. Pause or delay in my mind displays weakness—I feel a continuous need to be on my game.

I am fiercely independent and also—this one may surprise you—extremely self-conscious. I dislike scrutiny by others and even become defensive about it. I avoid confrontation and feel abused when forced to deal with others' lack of consideration or boundaries.

God calls me, though, to be a disciple to others ("Make disciples of other nations"). Problem is, I can barely manage to disciple myself. And therein, ironically, lies both the problem and the solution.

Jesus tells me that if I remain in Him and He in me I can bear fruit. Apart from Him I can do nothing. Why, then, am I so full of self-determination? Why do I still feel this compulsion to do it all on my own, to arrange and plan for everything? To avoid situations and take detours when fears overwhelm me?

Who's driving this bus, anyway?

Darkness Before the Dawn

The trials and tribulations of daily life had, by now, taken an immense toll on my heart and mind. The continuous diligence involved in recovery, owning and operating an expansive behavioral health company, the death of my mother, the resultant guardianship of my aunt and the spiritual surgery I seemed to be undergoing became overwhelming. I was thrust into a prolonged season of anxiety and depression.

Though still able to function, any down time in my schedule left me experiencing a vast distance from the usual salve of optimism and satisfaction that kept me energized. All of my accomplishments, values and desires seem to go stale in my heart. I've been a goal-oriented man, often driven and frequently taking inventory of what I had and where I was going in life. There seemed to be an incessant need in me to prepare for that "next" thing. So you can imagine my consternation upon failing to find satisfaction in any of my surroundings or accomplishments. I felt waves of despair and confusion rippling through my mind at inopportune times. My heart was heavy and sad. Yet still somehow I felt God was in it. Not necessarily causing it all, but walking with me through it. My morning devotions and quiet time were extended sessions of kneeling or lying down, tearful, pleading, releasing to God all of the unnamed discords and disconnects of my broken heart and life.

Thomas Keating, a Cistercian monk, refers to the desert experience of the fourth-century St. Anthony, which he refers to as "The Night of Sense." This is a profound experience whereby the usual senses on which we rely for assurance that all is well with God are suddenly diminished, leaving us in the uncomfortable disquiet of our own fears and uncertainties. The idols of self-reliance, control and certitude are exposed for the counterfeits they are, and we're left in a dark cave to grope our way through the hours and days, waiting and hoping for a source of light, escape and relief. This experience is not only extremely disorienting but laden with overwhelming emotion.

I didn't know any of this at the time I began experiencing these disconcerting periods. My friends and allies provided prayer and an empathetic ear, which really helped me to learn to release self-reliance. Still there was no clear answer as to what was happening to me. Even at this juncture I can only describe the results these symptoms had on me over the next 24 months. These included:

a. a breakthrough in dealing with negative patterns of attitude and behavior that I hadn't previously been able to achieve.
b. a strong attraction to people, as opposed to tasks.
c. a deeper empathy for others, along with a reduction in my judgmentalism and dogmatic reactions to people's problems.
d. a loss of my characteristic drivenness and a new attraction to extended periods of stillness in the company of God/nature.

e. validation and assurance that I was a good man who was unconditionally loved, and even delighted in, by God.
f. a persuasion that spiritual warfare is real.

This was the point at which I heard and responded—again reluctantly—by making the decision to enter the seminary. This was my response at this stage to being obedient to God's calling, coupled with the pull of that question "Why do I believe what I believe?" For three years I engaged in rigorous academic work and gained through it both a greater understanding of Christian doctrine and a deeper reliance upon God, especially in terms of venturing into unknown challenges.

While I had no intention of entering into formal ministry, I remained open to what God might have planned through this experience. I continued to participate in para-ministry activities with Ransomed Heart and other affiliates, spoke at men's breakfasts and preached occasional Sunday sermons when invited. I always enjoyed speaking and working in group settings, and the experience of living in the Good News was always something I could be passionate about. Still, I hesitated to submit to the transparency and demands of formal ministry. I know the cost of this life and have no romanticized conceptions about wearing the collar.

On the cold, snowy morning of December 5, 2011, I had another encounter with Jesus, who evidently likes to chat in the midst of busy deadlines. He can be playfully disruptive, but in this case He approached with some burning questions that needed answering. As is always the case, the answers were for my benefit. The events and dialogue, all of which will look familiar, went something like this:

Setting: Hotel room, Colorado Springs, Colorado
Time: 5:00 a.m.
Context: Just finished a four-day retreat at Advanced Wild at Heart Boot camp and am intending to catch the 6:30 a.m. flight back home. I'm mouthing a quick prayer before I head out the door for the airport.

Jesus: "Hold on a minute—I want you to stay here with me a little longer."

Jeff: "Okay, Lord" *(I move from kneeling to sitting).*

Jesus: "Jeff, do you really love me?"

Jeff: (*Oh boy!*) "Yes, Lord, you know that I do, . . . and I know where this is going!" *(tears)*

Jesus: "Feed my sheep. Jeff, do you love me with all of your heart, soul and life?"

Jeff: "Yes, Lord, I do, with all of me, with everything I am, with everything you'll make me. I can't do this by myself. You'll have to do this. I don't have what it takes; only you do."

(Jesus is exposing my hesitancy and reluctance to commit to a life of ministry. I've been processing this with other pastors and friends. I know my hesitancy and have been open about it to God and others. The crux of the problem is that I've hidden behind confusion instead of going with the certitude of obedience. My fig leaf is falling off, and we both know it.)

Jesus: "Do you really love me?"

Jeff: *(bunch of tears)* "Yes, Lord—*please* take these: I give you my reluctance, my self-determination, my fear and feelings of inadequacy. If you'll provide, if you'll make the call, I'll do whatever you ask. I love you, I worship you. You're my God and my King, my rescuer and my salvation. I live for you and repent of my fear."

Jesus: "Care for my lambs."

Jeff: "Yes, Lord."

Silence, peace. I get the sense that all has been said and that we're done for now. Our talk will continue to stir my heart, but I'm released to catch that plane home. It's finished, over and done with; my hesitation is removed and I'm open to whatever call might come—both now and until I die.

Reflection Questions

This chapter provides an intimate glimpse into a personal experience and encounter that would lead toward the pathway of expanded spiritual growth and breakthrough.

1. What sorts of defense mechanisms (be honest—we all have them) have you erected around your heart and life? That is, how do you avoid being placed in situations for which you don't already know the outcome? Or in which you're pretty sure you can't perform well?
2. List three to five methods (each) you use or have used to control:
   a. People
   b. Places
   c. Situations
3. What are your thoughts about the author's encounter with Jesus? Was this real or imagined? Explain your answer.
4. How do you handle the tough questions about faith, God and the meaning of life? Do you tend to brush them aside for a more opportune time? Or do you pursue dialogue, study and time with God to explore possible answers?

25

PUTTING IT ALL IN THE REARVIEW MIRROR

By 2011 October Road had become the area's largest provider of essential mental health services and the second largest provider of substance abuse services. We had begun to expand into adjacent counties and were eying some opportunities across the state of North Carolina. With an annual revenue approaching $5 million, we were poised for continued growth and success.

By the age of 50 I had experienced what may be called *success* on many levels—not the least of these the company's performance. But there was a growing emptiness, a longing for greater authenticity that couldn't be filled through the medium of behavioral health. My recent encounter with Jesus exposed that fact.

I had given consideration to selling the company before this point, but only on the basis of fear or frustration. Now the idea seemed logical, good. I contacted a healthcare broker whom I'd seen in one of the numerous advertisements that saturate every professional industry. Our conversations evolved into a feasibility study and, later, a valuation.

The rest, as they say, is history. After a brief marketing effort we entered into an intense season of due diligence with a prospective buyer. I had limited potential interests—only in those whose organizations had demonstrated a strong performance in terms of ethical and competent characteristics. If we sold, I wanted our good work and reputation to continue.

On April 30, 2012, October Road Incorporated, founded upon the remote dream of a disappointed and dejected middle manager, quietly sold in a multi-million dollar transaction. The vocational door of behavioral health was closed for me, and a new venture in Christian ministry began to materialize.

In his book *Can God be Trusted?—Faith and the Challenges of Evil* author John G. Stackhouse Jr. responds to the larger question of "Why Christianity?":

We long for immortality, we ache over our sins, we grieve over our losses, we mourn for the dead, we aspire for significance—all of these feelings, so deep and so upsetting that we only acknowledge them in life's most extreme experiences, are intimations of truth, according to the Christian faith. We may seek and often do seek to fill these holes in our psyches with sex or money or friendships or power or work or family. Or we deny them, lock them away, cut them off and destroy authentic parts of our deepest selves. "Our hearts are restless until we find our rest in thee," Augustine prayed. Blaise Pascal recognized the "God shaped vacuum" in every person's heart, a vacuum that sucks everything we use to stop it and remains unfilled. Christianity says *Yes!* to our desire to live forever, *Yes!* To our recognition that we are currently unfit to live forever, *Yes!* To our need for forgiveness and restoration, *Yes!* To our permanent attachment to loved ones, *Yes!* To our ambition to count for something that lasts, *Yes!* To our fundamental feeling that we are, in fact, utterly dependent upon God and that that is right. The Bible says, "in [Jesus] every one of God's promises is a *Yes!* (2 Corinthians 1:20). At the heart's core, Christianity makes sense. (p. 172)

It does and it has. God has brought me full circle back into the religion of my youth. The lens of clarity is sharpened by the experiences of this life, tried within the fires of this journey. But to one thing I can attest with absolute certainty: He has never taken His hand from me. Even though I'm imperfect and especially when I'm weak. I respond because I need and want to—and, more to the point, because I'm compelled to. Not from fear but from deep desire. Authenticity. Life. Love.

Reflection Questions

This chapter discuses the marketing and sale of the company and offers a brief discourse on why Christianity is a—no, let's make that *the* only—logical and beneficial choice.

1. Now that you've followed the story this far, what thoughts or feelings do you have about the outcome? What do you think would have happened if the author had never stepped out in risk and started the business?
2. What is your definition of Christianity? Are you willing to explore this further?

Application Exercise

If you're interested in exploring authentic and genuine Christianity as *the* valid means of living, or if your current Christianity isn't producing the life and freedom you're seeking, I suggest this reading: *Waking the Dead* by John Eldredge. You can also go to www.ransomedheart.com for other helpful resources in this area.

26

CLOSURE

Christian D. Larson was born on a farm near Forest City, Iowa, in February 1874, the fourth in a family of eight. His parents were born in Bergen, Norway.

As a boy he worked on the farm and attended country school. He later attended Iowa State College for two years and at the age of 22 began lecture work along psychological subjects.

A prolific writer, he has written much inspirational literature, in addition to his editorial writing and lecture work. At present, he divides his time between lecture work and writing at his home in Beverly Hills, California.

When asked what inspired him in composing the Optimist Creed, Mr. Larson has stated that "I wish I could tell you what inspired the writing of the lines "Promise Yourself," but there was nothing in particular; *it was just the product of a mind animated continuously by a deep desire to write something helpful."*

("The Author of the Optimist Creed," reprinted from the February 1944 issue of THE OPTIMIST Magazine, www.optimist.org/e/member/story_2013_125.cfm.)

It has taken nearly two years (as of this writing) to transition from the sale of the company into a life dedicated to ministry. This is an entirely different vocation, at least from the perspective of how it is approached.

Then there's the matter of another transition—moving into lifelong commitment. The past 23 years have included at least 15 geographical moves, a dozen employer changes and membership in six different churches. While most of these transitions were directed toward improving our lives, they have also created an undesirable byproduct of distant and/or seemingly disposable relationships.

The time and proximity it takes to really know people and be known by them can't efficiently be replicated over and over again. This process takes what it takes—time well spent in deep and meaningful conversations. This must happen naturally, in the context of the rhythms and circumstances of daily life. The more this occurs, the more we come to know and be known. The process is beautiful and messy all at the same time.

It's easy to keep things superficial. When we disagree or are annoyed by someone, our natural response can be to dismiss the offender from our circle and replace the person with another superficial friend. Or to just quit with all of it for a while—to do life, at least for a season, on our own. This applies in multiple settings: e.g., in a church or community or with a spouse. It's our consumerist mentality that drives this idea. In the end we end up hurting others and finding ourselves in a chronic state of loneliness and isolation.

Truth is, though, that we were made for relationship. And friendship can be deceptively difficult: it takes commitment, courage and sacrifice. The Benedictine Monks address this issue through a vow of stability—essentially an agreement to live out life within the community into which God has called us.

No, it isn't easy. That means I have to forfeit my rights to choose, change or give up. I'm required to stay engaged—in and with the disappointment, frustration, inconvenience and occasional annoyance of who and what *you* are. This principle applies to my friends, my church and my community.

When you do the same we both come to know acceptance. And through acceptance we experience love—love that heals, invites, nurtures and soothes, fulfills, removes the felt need for falseness and eliminates fear.

The return on this investment is exponential. I find and experience belonging, purpose and peace. I witness the faithfulness of God working things out within my field of vision. And in conjunction with that I experience strengthened faith and enhanced freedom.

My vow of stability is a work in progress. It started with returning yet again to my hometown of Charleston, South Carolina. It has involved a return to the friendships that were initiated more than two decades ago. It has included choosing to live in a home older than I am—a reminder that life precedes and continues beyond me. It has meant living in the same community in which I grew up, allowing me to retrace the steps I took as a boy and thereby reminding me of the good and the bad aspects of those days. It has entailed walking in a new identity and in the truth that God does work out all things for the good of those who love Him. It has involved agreeing that I will remain here for the rest of my days, that I won't again either run or relocate. It has entailed coming full circle to where it all started, with a mission to participate in community, life and love.

The story of this life has been reinterpreted through the lens of redemption and restoration. I am grateful and indebted to the family and friends who provided the emotional space and resources I needed to grow. My mother was a source of encouragement and faith in my life. She held to a posture of humility and quiet strength and demonstrated deep character through her perseverance, work ethic and mental toughness. My siblings each contributed something positive along the way. My sister loved unconditionally, my brothers gave masculine strength and validation. My spouse has rescued my heart, through and through. The fellowship of recovery has cultivated maturity and wisdom for my soul. God has remained true.

It's with this intent that I've devoted my best effort to recalling and conveying the experiences that have comprised a life lived in both adversity and victory. I hope this book has been helpful. If I've accomplished my mission, then the story of God's loving and faithful character has been imprinted upon your heart. My hope is that you'll hear the invitation and sense the unquenchable love of God both in the narrative and in the context of your own life story. My wish is that it will take root in your soul and nourish your dreams and desires, that it will encourage you to come fully alive in the Good News that is the gospel.

I look forward to continuing with you on this path that encompasses the journey of life, here in the present. Maybe we'll get to chat sometime. I'm always intrigued to hear about the good things God is up to in another's life. If we don't meet, just look around. God is actively engaged everywhere and with so many people. Let their story and the testimony of their lives instill within you the hope—and hopefully ultimately the assurance—that God is in love with you, that He went so far as to bleed Himself for you. He gave that life by dying within an undying love.

Until the time we may meet, please accept and bask in one of my favorite blessings:

The LORD bless you and keep you;
the LORD make his face to shine upon you and be gracious to you;
the LORD lift up his countenance upon you and give you peace.
(Numbers 6:24–26, ESV)

Jeff R. Brooks
Charleston, South Carolina
August 2013

Reflection Questions

This chapter opens with a newspaper article from years ago that recounts the story of the author of the creed for Optimist Club International, reflecting Jefferey Brooks's own motive for writing. It also encourages and invites the reader to reflect upon this story and upon their own lives, dreams and desires; to explore their respective beliefs as to who God is; and to launch into the freedom that is available in relationship with Him.

1. What are your thoughts about this story?
2. What are your feelings about this story?
3. What have you learned from the story?
4. How will you apply any lessons you've gained?

ABOUT THE AUTHOR

Jeff R. Brooks is a writer, student, and pastor living in Charleston, South Carolina, with his wife and best friend, Robin, who has been a constant encourager and source of strength throughout his redemptive journey. They are the proud and loving parents of two adult children.

Jeff holds an undergraduate degree in psychology from Limestone College, a graduate degree in healthcare administration from the University of South Carolina, and a Certificate of Christian Studies from Asbury Theological Seminary, where he is currently enrolled in the Doctor of Ministry program.

Jeff has an extensive background in the treatment of mental health and substance abuse disorders, serving children, adolescents, and adults over a twenty-year career. He holds state licensure as a substance abuse specialist, an advance certification in relapse prevention, national certification as a master addiction counselor, and board certification in healthcare management through the American College of Healthcare Executives.

Jeff and his wife founded and operated a highly successful behavioral healthcare business that they recently sold to respond to the call of ministry. They spend their time enjoying the low country waterways, fellowshipping with seekers and new believers, and spending extensive periods watching college football.

3 DAYS RISING

Jeff Brooks is president and co-founder of 3 Days Rising, a 501(c)3 nonprofit organization dedicated to promoting God's intimate and restorative love to every human being. Proceeds from this book will be used to support the work of this organization. To learn more about the mission, please visit www.3daysrising.com.